On the Road: Surviving Divorce

Sheryl Garrett, CFP®
Series Editor

Adapted and compiled by
Ruth J. Mills

Dearborn™
Trade Publishing
A **Kaplan Professional** Company

This publication is designed to provide accurate and authoritative information
in regard to the subject matter covered. It is sold with the understanding that the
publisher is not engaged in rendering legal, accounting, or other professional service.
If legal advice or other expert assistance is required, the services of a competent
professional person should be sought.

President, Dearborn Publishing: Roy Lipner
Vice President and Publisher: Cynthia A. Zigmund
Senior Acquisitions Editor: Mary B. Good
Cover Design: Design Solutions

Published by Dearborn Trade Publishing
A Kaplan Professional Company

A Stonesong Press Book

Project Manager: Ellen Schneid Coleman
Interior Design: Brad Walrod/High Text Graphics, Inc.

Printed in the United States of America

06 07 08   10 9 8 7 6 5 4 3 2 1

Library of Congress Cataloging-in-Publication Data
Surviving divorce/edited by Sheryl Garrett; adapted and
compiled by Ruth J. Mills.
      p.   cm.—(On the road)
   Includes index.
   ISBN 1-4195-0041-4 (5 × 7.375 pbk.)
   1. Divorced people—Finance, Personal.   I. Garrett, Sheryl.
II. Mills, Ruth J.   III. On the road (Chicago, Ill.)
HG179.S863 2006
332.024'0086'53—dc22   2005022391

Dearborn Trade books are available at special quantity discounts to use for sales
promotions, employee premiums, or educational purposes. Please call our Special
Sales Department to order or for more information at 800-621-9621, ext. 4444, e-mail
trade@dearborn.com, or write to Dearborn Trade Publishing, 30 South Wacker Drive,
Suite 2500, Chicago, IL 60606-7481.

Contents

Introduction

On the Road: Surviving Divorce is part of a new series of books from Dearborn Trade Publishing intended to help you deal with the financial issues, problems, and decisions concerning specific life events. The financial decisions you face when you're getting divorced are, obviously, different from the decisions you made when you were getting married or when just starting out in life.

Financial planning shouldn't be intimidating. So we've created these books to take away the terror. *On the Road* books are like travel guides to help you make the best financial decisions at each stage of your life—in this case, for surviving divorce. For most people, divorce is a very painful journey, but this book can help you make the necessary decisions rationally, so you can divide your property fairly and make sure you have the money you need for the next phase of your life. Therefore, this book addresses the issues that concern you *now*:

- ▶ hiring an attorney to handle your divorce—or using arbitration or mediation instead;
- ▶ dividing up all your assets, including your home and everything else you own;
- ▶ dividing up your pension and retirement savings plans, and updating your retirement plans after you're divorced;
- ▶ making decisions about alimony and child support, and knowing what you need to about the tax implications of both—whether you're receiving or paying;
- ▶ getting a handle on the change in income, assets, liabilities, expenses, and investments—and making a new budget for your new solo lifestyle; and
- ▶ making new financial plans for after your divorce.

These financial decisions are part of your life's journey, so we've made them easy to navigate, with lots of helpful "Roadmaps" (charts and tables of financial information to help you with each issue or decision that comes up) and "Tollbooths" that help you calculate your expenses or savings, as well as

"Hazard" signs that caution you on money pitfalls to watch out for. We've included "What to Pack" so you'll know what forms or other information you need to get a mortgage, for example. There are "Postcards" that tell helpful stories of how other people have made their financial journey successfully.

Finally, we've included an "Itinerary," a recap of all the key actions you should take—all of which are covered in detail in the six chapters of this book. At the end we have included a list of other books and resources you could turn to if you want more in-depth information on such topics as finding certified divorce financial analysts and qualified lawyers, mediators, or arbitrators, and handling credit problems.

We hope you find this travel guide helpful as you map your route to financial success and peace of mind during and after this difficult time. Remember, your life is an adventure, and money paves the way. So let's get started on making sure you get what you need for this part of your life's journey.

Paying Tolls

Hiring an Attorney vs. Mediation/Arbitration

There are three basic routes to getting a divorce: You can hire an attorney, go through mediation or arbitration (both of which involve a neutral third party), or do it yourself (which is *not* recommended; we'll explain why at the end of the chapter). In this chapter, we'll discuss the differences among these three routes and what you need to know about the financials of each. Before we get into details, though, let's take a quick look at which route works best for different situations.

Do you need an attorney? In a nutshell, we would say yes. But there are exceptions. In most states, you *can* get a divorce without a lawyer. If you choose to go this do-it-yourself route, be aware that successfully handling a divorce without a lawyer requires certain key emotional and legal conditions. You can consider *not using* a lawyer if:

▶ You feel that you and your spouse have approximately equal emotional power in your relationship (in contrast, if you feel that your spouse has greater power, then you may want the stronger representation that a divorce attorney can provide);

▶ You both know what your rights are and will (and do) stand up for your rights;

▶ You both have track records of being fair and honest;

▶ Both can agree on every issue;

▶ You have no significant property, such as a house, business, or pension plan, to divide;

▶ You have no children to provide for; and

▶ There will be no alimony for either party.

If this sounds like you and your spouse, then congratulate yourselves on saving money on legal fees. There are several do-it-yourself books available to assist you through the process. If this doesn't describe your situation, continue reading the rest of this chapter, which focuses on the other two routes. Let's start with the most traveled road: working with an attorney.

Hazard!

Who's Driving?

▶ Beware if the decision *not* to use a lawyer is driven by the spouse with power in the relationship to destroy the weaker partner.

▶ Remember, a lawyer can only represent *one* of you; *not* you and your spouse "jointly."

▶ Experience *does* matter. Let the new lawyer learn the ropes at *someone else's* expense, not yours.

▶ Route 1: Hiring a "Driver": A Qualified, Experienced Divorce Attorney

Legal representation is critical in any divorce that involves assets and/or children. How you hire and manage an attorney will have a substantial impact on your checkbook. Besides you and your spouse, your attorney is the primary player in your divorce. As a rule, your attorney will be the conductor, orchestrating various sections of your "divorce advisory team" as your divorce moves along. As we'll see in later chapters, your team might include real estate appraisers (to help you determine the value of your home or other property), business appraisers (if you or your spouse own a business), financial consultants (such as CPAs, certified financial planners, or certified divorce financial analysts), insurance agents, pension plan evaluators, and perhaps therapists for you or your kids, if you have any.

Let's start out by focusing on the leader of that team, the attorney. We'll cover costs, questions to ask, and how to work most effectively with your attorney.

Hire Your Own "Driver": You and Your Spouse Should Have Separate Attorneys

In most cases, it is almost a conflict of interest for you to use the same attorney. For example, Samantha Williams gained an extra $15,000 after hiring her own attorney. She had tried to work with a friend who agreed to help her and her husband settle their divorce. When Samantha hired her own attorney, the first interview revealed that the equity in her home had been determined by calculating the difference between the *original cost* of the house and its current market value, which was all wrong: Equity is determined by the difference between *present mortgage(s)* and current market value.

The $15,000 Samantha gained might seem like small change to some people, but consider the story of another person who left more than $1 million on the table because her attorney (and good friend) said he wouldn't handle the couple's divorce (jointly) if there was any bickering over assets. So whether you can save $15,000, $1 million, or just a few hundred dollars, you are strongly advised to have your own advocate. Not necessarily one who is *adversarial*, but one who owes allegiance only to *you*.

Although one lawyer can never really represent both you and your spouse, it isn't always necessary to have two lawyers. If your situation is simple and there are no contested issues, one of the parties can appear *pro se*, that is, represent one's own self. In that case, one lawyer draws up all the necessary documents and proceeds with the dissolution, eliminating the necessity of a second lawyer. Still, if you are going to "share" a lawyer, make it clear who that lawyer's client is.

A word of caution: If your divorce involves regular support payments; questions over custody or visitation of children; or division of property, you should at least have a second lawyer look over the agreement before you sign it. A small change in the weekly support rate can mean thousands of dollars over an extended period. A misunderstanding about your interest in marital property could result and create an unexpected tax obligation, and so on. Only in the most basic cases should you consider going it alone—and perhaps not even then.

Who's the Right "Driver"? Where to Look for the Best Attorney for You

Rarely will you find the right attorney by simply calling the local bar association for the recommended list of the month. Instead, try to get a referral from a close friend who went through a divorce.

Unfortunately, that isn't always possible. You may be able to get plenty of referrals for attorneys, but usually they come from friends who dealt with attorneys on real estate deals or in drawing up wills. Family law and divorce are highly specialized fields. Choose someone in that field and who specializes primarily in family law, who dedicates a minimum of 50 percent of the practice to divorce, and who has at least five years' experience. If the attorney doesn't have these three prerequisites, take a pass.

There is a lot to be learned and plenty of mistakes that can be made. Open your ears: you will be surprised what your friends, next-door neighbors, and co-workers share about their catastrophes as well as successes. Pay close attention to the catastrophes—they can shorten your learning curve.

It is very important to have a top-notch attorney. Don't interview one or more attorneys, find someone who answers all your questions with flying colors, and then reject the person because you feel that lawyer's too expensive. There are horror stories of people who hire cheap attorneys and end up in a mess. Very often three or four years later, they hobble back to the "expensive" attorney they passed up, to straighten out the mess created by the less experienced and less sophisticated counsel they had hired to handle the divorce. They usually come up with, "Oh, I wish I had kept you in the beginning. You were right. I didn't follow your advice and went to a cheap lawyer and got cheap work done." But remember, repentance might not really help here. The original attorney would rarely take on such cases. It's not venegeance or ego, but a factor of the law of diminishing returns. Most of the damage has already been done and is irreparable. The bottom line is: Don't be penny wise and pound foolish. Hire a top-notch attorney: every penny spent on this "expensive" attorney would be worth it.

Specialist vs. Generalist

A lawyer does not necessarily have to be a divorce specialist, but if you have a choice, you should strongly consider using one. The minimum that you should look for in your lawyer is familiarity with the rules of procedure and practice used in the court where your case will be heard. Choosing an attorney is similar to choosing a doctor: If you have a complex medical problem, you are more likely to go to a specialist than a general practitioner. If your case is simple and on the borderline between needing and not needing a lawyer at all, you have less of a need for a specialist, but if your case is potentially complex or contested, go for a specialist. Even in simple cases, your lawyer can give you perspective about possible outcomes.

If you are seeking alimony (or are going to pay it) or if you have children who will require financial support, your lawyer must be familiar with the support ranges and property divisions customarily granted in your court. Changing laws and changing judges result in changing applications of the law. A novice or someone who doesn't keep up with changes in family law can easily sabotage your case.

Hazard!
What You Don't Know about Taxes Can Kill You

Knowledge of tax law is a must where property transfers and support payments are involved. You need a divorce lawyer who can foresee potential problems and make their resolution a part of the settlement. If necessary, look beyond your lawyer for tax expertise to assist in the resolution.

Your choice of an attorney may also be influenced by your spouse's decision. If you suspect your spouse has hired or will hire a lawyer with considerable experience who carries a great deal of weight in the court, you need a lawyer with equal influence. The consideration that your case and your lawyer will receive is very often related to the respect your lawyer can command from the court and the opposing lawyer.

For example, one woman said her husband decided to settle the case when he saw the car her lawyer was driving. He told her, "I thought you were going to have a beat-up, used-car lawyer, but when you showed up with a Ferrari lawyer, I figure I was beaten already." Although this woman's lawyer had an impact on her spouse, don't choose a lawyer based on your assumption of how your spouse will react. Choose one who will have a positive impact on your spouse's *lawyer*. If your spouse has a lawyer, there will be little, if any, interaction between your lawyer and your spouse.

Hazard!

Where Not to Look for a Divorce Lawyer

There are a number of ways not to choose a lawyer:

▶ Do not ask a lawyer to handle your case if that person is not a divorce lawyer.

▶ Do not choose the lawyer who handled your parent's estate, who helped you prepare your wills, who handles the business law issues you or your spouse face, or who handled the real estate closing on your house to handle the divorce. These areas of the law are *not* a substitute for divorce law experience.

▶ Do not ask an attorney friend to take your case—you'll both end up regretting it. If you ask a friend to take your case, the person might do so only because of your friendship. Don't put your friend in this position.

▶ Do not call an attorney who has handled legal problems for your spouse in the past.

Because lawyers are now permitted to advertise, as a last resort you can look in your local newspaper or Yellow Pages to find a lawyer who specializes in divorce law. Some states have a process of legal specialization in which lawyers can be certified as specialists in certain fields of law. This process is demanding and screens out those who have a passing interest in the field. If your state certifies specialists, concentrate on these specialists. Unfortunately, most states do *not* certify specialists, and there is no way to verify the truth of any particular advertisement without checking into that lawyer's reputation through the bar association or by asking other lawyers or friends who have dealt with the person.

If you have a referral source in whom you have total confidence, see that lawyer first. For example, if you have a great deal of trust in your business lawyer who makes a very strong recommendation, see that person first. Then

Roadmap 1.1

Where to Look for a Divorce Lawyer

As mentioned, your best sources of attorneys will be personal referrals:

▶ Ask an attorney you have used—and liked—for a recommendation.
▶ Ask friends and relatives who have dealt with divorce lawyers. (Because no one ever feels like a winner in a divorce, they may even refer you to their spouse's lawyer!) In any event, they can tell you about their own experience with their lawyer and give you some help on what to look for and what to avoid. Listen to divorce stories from friends and colleagues. Ask the following questions, preferably from someone who is at least two years postdivorce:
▶ What kind of settlement did you get?
▶ What areas were settled fairly and quickly?
▶ If you went through another divorce, would you hire this attorney again?
▶ Overall, were you happy with how the case was handled?
▶ Did the attorney's efforts interfere with or even jeopardize whatever relationship existed with your spouse?
▶ Did you feel you were kept informed, or kept in the dark?
▶ Did you feel comfortable with your attorney?
▶ In hindsight, did the fees paid and the overall results from the divorce seem fair?
▶ Check the referral services of your state and local bar associations, listed in the telephone Yellow Pages. Tell them it is a divorce case and ask for the names of a couple of people experienced in that area of practice. On a national level, if you want to find an exceptionally qualified and experienced divorce lawyer, call the headquarters for the American Academy of Matrimonial Lawyers in Chicago at 312-263-6477 for referrals in your area.
▶ You can always call the local courts and ask for the name of the presiding judge for family law. Then, ask to speak to the judge's law clerk. The judge would probably not talk to you, but the law clerk may be open with information about where to look for an attorney.
▶ Consult the *Martindale-Hubble Directory*, found in most large libraries. Remember, however, that the information found in this text is provided by the lawyers for a fee—and it's a little like looking in the Yellow Pages for an attorney (see below), which is not really the best way to find someone to handle such a personal and emotional situation as divorce.
▶ Don't forget the Internet search engines if you use a computer and are online. If you don't have a computer, your local library does. Again, though, keep in mind that this is a very generic approach to searching for a lawyer; a personal recommendation from friends or other professionals is a better way to find a qualified lawyer with whom you'll feel comfortable working.

interview at least two more attorneys and compare them in terms of competence, personality, and price. A lawyer's reputation among other lawyers is probably the most valid indication of their capabilities and weaknesses.

Be wary if your spouse suggests that you hire a particular lawyer. Ask yourself, "Is it likely my spouse wants me to have the best divorce lawyer in town—or even the tenth best?" But don't eliminate a particular lawyer who seems right for you just because of your spouse's recommendation—just make sure to check out that lawyer very carefully.

You should put a great deal of effort into finding a lawyer: it may be one of the most important decisions you make. The wrong choice can mean endless, painful, and expensive litigation; heartache; frustration; anger; and consequences you (and perhaps your children) will have to live with for the rest of your life.

Should You "Carpool"? Working with a Legal Clinic Instead of a Single Lawyer

One way to reduce costs is to use a legal clinic—a group of lawyers and paralegals who supply legal services at lower rates than the typical firm. The bottom line is that the clinic's quality of service will depend on the lawyers and paralegals involved. The difference between law clinics and private offices is that clinic lawyers attempt to minimize the number of hours spent with you, the client. Clinics maximize the use of forms and the assistance of secretaries and paralegals who are paid at lower rates than those with law degrees. This approach can be satisfactory if your case is simple and doesn't require a lot of contact between you and the lawyer.

Even if the price seems right, you still must consider the lawyer's competence and personality. Ask yourself, "If this lawyer is really as good, why is this person working for a clinic at one-fourth of the price of other, experienced lawyers?" If, after your initial interview, you are satisfied with the responses you get, there is no reason not to hire the lawyer. Your pocketbook may benefit.

Always ask whether that lawyer will be the person representing you, or whether it will be an associate or other office personnel. Many people have been quite surprised to find out that the person they interviewed ended up doing only a small amount of work on their divorces. If your case requires personal attention, then you want to know who will be giving you that attention.

Also know that just because a clinic may advertise a divorce for as low as $250 does not mean it won't be entitled to a larger fee if your case is more complicated and requires more time or court appearances. Therefore, you should always clarify payment terms at the outset of your relationship with the law clinic as with any other law office. *Never assume anything.*

Ask what the hourly charge for the clinic lawyer is and the expected total fee. Compare that rate with what is commonly charged in your community and determine whether the clinic is really the bargain you expected.

Don't Get Lost! Narrow Your Search for the Right Lawyer (to Avoid Hiring the Wrong One)

Your divorce (or any financial concern for that matter) is no place for on-the-job training. Keep in mind that, unlike doctors who work as interns and residents under close supervision, there is no similar requirement before lawyers can hang out a shingle. If you were lying on a stretcher in the emergency room after a car accident, you would want an experienced physician trained in emergency medical care, not a doctor who reads X-rays for a living. The same is true for your lawyer.

When making your decision about which lawyer to hire to handle your divorce, always consider the personality factor. You will have to work closely with your lawyer on potentially volatile and personal problems. Although there doesn't need to be a perfect match, if your personalities clash, it can make this relationship uncomfortable or even contentious.

If your case is simple, avoid a lawyer who appears to be unnecessarily combative or egoistic. There is too much on your plate already; all you want is a good result. Lawyers with big egos or bad attitude could turn a simple inexpensive case into a long expensive struggle that could cost you big bucks. To some degree, you should rely on your instincts.

The following character descriptions should show you what you *do not* want in a lawyer. Think about them when you interview attorneys. Divorce can be expensive, so you want to spend your money wisely.

"Trust me, leave it all to me." This "father-knows-best" (or "mother-knows-best") type of lawyer dismisses your questions and concerns. This lawyer may appear to offer you options as the case goes along but will probably try to manipulate you into approving their decisions.

"On the one hand ...; on the other hand ..." At the other extreme is this wishy-washy lawyer who will never express an opinion about anything. You will not get a straight answer no matter how hard you try. Over and over again, this lawyer will tell you that nothing is predictable, and anything can happen. Favorite phrases are, "We'll check that out," or "Let's see about that," or "There's no way of telling."

"Which way to the battlefield?" Rambo lawyers look at every issue as an opportunity to use everything from martial arts to nuclear bombs. Most of this enthusiasm probably will be directed at your soon-to-be-ex-spouse, but you may need your own ninja if you disagree on some part of this lawyer's strategy or tactics. Unfortunately, this confrontational style may cause the other side to dig in its heels and turn your divorce into a bitter and expensive mother of all battles. Frequently these lawyers use the experience to build their egos—at your expense.

"Where do we sign and which way to the back door?" This marshmallow will avoid conflict at all costs, is always ready to settle every question, and readily sees the reasons and justifications of the other side. This lawyer will try to avoid a trial at all costs. You will be lucky to leave your marriage with the clothes on your back. And if your case ever comes to trial, forget about having this person fight for your rights.

"Hold that thought . . . Isn't call waiting wonderful?" A visit to this center of the universe is a real treat. This lawyer is always talking on the phone while the intercom keeps buzzing. A stack of unanswered messages is always in a pile on the desk. During your interview, there will be calls and "urgent" interruptions parading through the office. If you are lucky, this lawyer may hear a word or two that you say and will manage to give you a word or two in response before sending you out the door.

"I am your knight in shining armor." Sir Galahad takes the view that law is a secret world that only they can understand. Certainly, a layperson could never appreciate what this lawyer does and how they can orchestrate your case. Don't expect any information on the details or strategy of your case —only wait to be told where to sign and what to say. You will not be given any options, just this lawyer's opinion.

"Did you see me on the evening news?" The celebrity lawyer is a master at self-promotion and more interested in looking good for the press and public than in obtaining a good result for you.

"Oh, you poor dear." Nurse lawyer bleeds right along with you. This lawyer will see to it that you use lots of Kleenex® during your visits. In the end, you will have gotten more faulty therapy than competent legal advice.

Rest Stop: Avoid Overloaded Attorneys

Let's face it: most of us today are overloaded. Your attorney is no different. A common post-divorce complaint is that clients feel their attorneys didn't fully pay attention to critical issues and that, at times, their cases were not managed well.

Many attorneys take on more cases than they can really manage, in the same way that airlines overbook. They know that some of their cases will eventually drop out, some will settle, some of the parties will change their minds and reconcile, and some cases will take longer than originally anticipated. To compensate for these fluctuations, many attorneys fill up their pipelines with too many clients. In the end, it becomes a way of life for them. If this is a concern for you, get it out on the table now.

Therefore, this is the time to be proactive. You need to take the bull by the horns and force an attorney you're interviewing to respond when you ask a question along the line of:

▶ What happens when a court date is scheduled?
▶ What happens when the tax returns are delivered?
▶ What happens when we bring the appraiser in to evaluate the business?
▶ What happens when . . .?

Some attorneys will duck, waffle, equivocate, and otherwise refuse to answer the questions. Pin down the attorney, to narrow the field before you hire one. If you ask, "When will my case go to trial?" and the attorney responds, "A long time from now," you, in turn can respond by specifying: "Would you say, within one year from today?" If the attorney responds, "Oh, before then," you know you have the furthest-out time or drop-dead date. You can then counter with, "Would you say, within the next six months?" If the answer is "No. Not that soon," you now have a six-month period where you have some idea when this will be going to trial, if it does. You can then respond, "Now I know approximately when it will go to trial. What has to happen prior to that time and what will happen during? Let's work backward so I understand it." In other words, you need to say, "Give me the game plan."

Find out the order in which the events will happen. If the attorney can't answer, you are better off leaving and finding a different attorney. If the attorney responds, "I really can't tell you what will happen, but I can give you some guidelines," that's great—it becomes part of your game plan.

After the attorney gives you some guidelines, write them down and send a letter back saying the following:

"This is my understanding of our discussion. These are the things that will happen: [fill in the blank]. I know you can't quote exactly how much time and effort you will put into them, but please do not spend any amount of time in excess of your original dollar estimate without my authorization."

Never give an attorney open access to your bank account. Avoid, with fear of your financial life, someone who says, "Don't worry. I'll take care of everything. Just pay my bill when it arrives." You really need to get fee and hour estimates and an overview of the game plan. If the attorney has to go on a fishing expedition looking for assets and documents, you are going to be spending a lot of money.

Also, if you have combined known assets (that is, neither of you is in a position to have hidden-away money and/or that all your income and your spouse's comes from verifiable on-the books sources—i.e., not a cash business), and you have limited funds, why pay $400 an hour when you can get adequate and reliable representation for less? The key here is to ask around. Your local bar association can offer the average fee range in the area. The total fee for quality representation is the bottom line. Don't let hourly rates confuse the issue.

Bumps in the Road: What to Avoid When Deciding on a Lawyer

Still not sure about your prospective lawyer? Here is some final advice: Run, do not walk, out the door if, during the interview with a prospective lawyer, you hear any of the following:

▶ "I'll represent both you and your spouse. There is no reason for both of you to have a lawyer." As discussed earlier, one attorney cannot ethically represent both parties.

▶ "Mediation doesn't work, so don't waste your time." Mediation can and does work, and it should usually be attempted. We'll discuss mediation in more detail later in this chapter.

▶ "Tell you what: I'll charge you only a low, flat fee for your divorce." A lawyer who is not making a reasonable fee probably will not put all into your case.

▶ "I promise you . . ." Nothing is certain in a divorce. Ever.

▶ "We will win this case." In the long run, a divorce is not about winning or losing, and a lawyer who believes that they have to win can be very expensive and often will push the other side into positions of unreasonableness.

▶ "I'll win the kids for you." The children are not property to be won or lost; neither should they be used as weapons.

Stop #1 on the Find-an-Attorney Journey: The Initial Interview

One of the important things to find out when you make an appointment with an attorney is whether they will charge you for the initial interview. But you had better be serious about working with that attorney. If they don't charge for the initial interview and it becomes clear that you are really there to obtain free information, the attorney will probably end the interview quickly.

So you've narrowed down your search, you know the key areas of the divorce process, and you have insight into the lawyer's turf. Here are some questions to ask a lawyer during your initial interview:

▶ What percentage of your practice involves divorce? (As mentioned above, you don't want an amateur. Look for someone who has specialized in family law for at least five years. This means that a minimum of 50 percent of their practice is dedicated to divorce.)

▶ Do you have trial experience in divorce cases, or do you usually settle out of court? What percent of your cases go to trial? (If you think this is where you are headed, you definitely want someone with experience in trial work.)

▶ Will you go to court to litigate the case if it cannot be settled?

▶ Do you consider yourself a litigator, negotiator, arbitrator, or mediator? (It depends on what you want. Do you want to negotiate a settlement or prepare for war?)

▶ Do you routinely represent clients in my county? (Never underestimate the old-boy or old-girl networks. Strangers are not always welcome.)

▶ Will you handle the case personally, or will an associate in your office handle it? (If another person is to be involved, you may wish to interview that person before retaining the lawyer. Also ask if there is a difference in rates, and how that will affect your total cost.)

▶ Do you charge extra for work done by paralegals or secretaries? (If the answer is yes, ask what their rates are; they should be lower.)

▶ What is your procedure for calling you outside of normal business hours if it is necessary?

▶ In this jurisdiction, approximately how long does it take to resolve this case if an agreement is reached? How long will it take if it must go to trial?

▶ What do you expect of me?

▶ How do you charge for your services? Please show me your fee agreement and explain it to me.

▶ Do you think your fees are average, above average, or below average for this area?

▶ Do you have a written contract or retainer agreement? Please show it to me and explain it. (The answer should be yes. It should state fee structures and the attorney's responsibility to you. If, at a later date, you decide to switch attorneys after signing an agreement, you can. An attorney cannot prevent you from taking your file elsewhere.)

▶ What do you estimate court costs will be?

▶ Which spouse will be liable for the fees and court costs? How will that be determined?

▶ Do you charge a retainer fee? How much will it be? Under what circumstances is it refundable in full or in part?

▶ Can you give a ballpark estimate on the total fee?

▶ Will there be monthly billings or will the fee be due at some particular time?

▶ Will there be charges for outside services by accountants or investigators? Will I be able to approve such services in advance?

▶ Based on the information I have given you, what results would you expect on any particular contested issue either by court decision or by negotiation? (Because predictions are risky and the information you have provided is probably incomplete, you should expect a guarded answer with no absolute assurances of a particular result.)

▶ (If you have kids): What's your attitude about joint or legal custody? (Make sure you probe and ask what has worked and what has not worked.)

▶ How do local laws affect any issues that may be contested, such as child custody, support, alimony, or property division?

▶ Are you an active member of family law committees in your local state or national bar association? Are you a member of the American Academy of Matrimonial Lawyers? (Answers should be yes.)

You should also ask any personal questions you have regarding your rights and responsibilities in connection with your spouse, e.g., whether you must continue to prepare meals if you both share the same house, pay your spouse's charge accounts, file joint tax returns, etc. And you may think of other questions you'd like to ask. If an answer to a question is not satisfactory or you do not understand it, say so immediately. Don't be afraid to show your lack of understanding. A good attorney wants to know when you do not understand aspects of your case. You are paying to know the answers to your questions and to have them explained thoroughly, but you must ask the right questions.

Some of these points and questions may seem overwhelming. But if you don't ask questions up front, you will regret it as time progresses. None of your questions are unimportant to you—that's why you are asking. Ask each one, write down the answers, and review them. They will form a bible for you.

The Road Ahead: What to Look for When Interviewing a Lawyer

Now that you know something about some of the personality types, experience (or the lack thereof), and behaviors you should *avoid* when choosing a lawyer, here are some things your lawyer *should* do:

▶ Listen attentively.

▶ Instill a sense of confidence based on expertise and experience on the issues you face.

▶ Provide you with options and explain the pros and cons of a particular course of action.

▶ Outline what you may realistically expect.

▶ Defend you vigorously to obtain every advantage you can get, including competent representation in a trial if that is necessary.

▶ Give you honest feedback when you are off track.

▶ Act as a peacemaker, when necessary, by explaining the benefits of negotiating terms that you and your spouse can accept.

▶ Have an active law practice from which you can benefit because of the lawyer's vast experience.

▶ Have a good reputation with the court and opposing counsel.

▶ Have an experienced and congenial support staff.

▶ Be sensitive enough to the inevitable emotional struggles facing you during your divorce.

▶ Help you maintain perspective as to what is a fair settlement.

▶ Conduct aggressive discovery of all assets and income.

▶ Significantly control the case—to the degree possible. Your lawyer should control *you* to avoid willful violations of court orders or agreements, and your lawyer should control *the opposition* by blocking attempts to take advantage of you.

▶ File all pleadings and motions in a timely fashion—and not on the last day permitted.

▶ Respect you and your ideas and suggestions.

Hazard!

Before You Hire ... Listen Carefully

When asking questions of your lawyer or a lawyer you're considering hiring, keep in mind that *people under stress are usually very poor listeners.* So when you ask your lawyer a question, *listen* to the answers rather than thinking ahead to your next question. Don't be afraid to take notes. Again, if you brought a list of questions, you don't have to think ahead to your next one. Hint: Write down the answers you are given. If unsure what your attorney said, ask for clarification. Most people think they heard and understood what was said. Then they find out that they really didn't.

Stay on Course: Four Key Areas to Discuss with Your Lawyer

Typically, during the first few meetings with a divorce attorney four types of questions pop up; of these you need to know which ones are important to you. A word of caution here: Some lawyers are going to become incredibly defensive when you start probing into "their" territory. After all, they're the experts, right? *Not necessarily.* Too many make mistakes—and your objective is to avoid mistakes.

One way to lead up to these questions is to say something like the following (feel free to memorize and use verbatim):

"Suppose your child needed brain surgery. I bet you would probe thoroughly into the surgeon's background and credentials before you would let the doctor operate, wouldn't you? Me too. Well, I'm new at divorce and I feel like I'm going through a major and radical surgery. I need to know everything before we proceed. My intention is not to micromanage my case, but I'm going to be an involved client."

With that said, here are the four topics you might want to discuss at the outset.

1. The Divorce Process. Here are some questions you should consider:

- ▶ Who pays the legal fees? (Sometimes your legal fees can come out of your settlement—which means your spouse may pay.)
- ▶ If you must take your ex to court for nonsupport or for not complying with the divorce decree, who pays the legal fees and court costs? Will there be interest charges?
- ▶ (If you are the wife), do you want to take back your maiden name? (This may affect your credit if your credit history is all under your married name).

2. Property. Consider these issues:

- ▶ Who gets which property?
- ▶ Who gets which debt?
- ▶ If the pension is to be divided, how is the division determined? Has the proper paperwork been prepared?
- ▶ If there is a property settlement note, is it collateralized? Is there interest on it?
- ▶ Does the spouse who gets the house get the whole basis in the house?
- ▶ If the spouse who gets the house needs to sell it immediately, will that person be responsible for the entire capital gains tax?
- ▶ Is the net after-tax value of the retirement plan, the house, any personal assets, and their respective appreciation potential taken into account?

3. **Alimony.** Consider these issues:

> ▶ How much alimony can you get (or will you have to pay), and for how long?
> ▶ If alimony is not awarded now, can it be awarded later?
> ▶ Will there be life insurance to cover alimony in the event of the payer's death? How can this be verified?

4. **Child support.** These are the questions clients typically ask:

> ▶ How much child support will be paid, and for how long?
> ▶ Will the child support change during college or when visitation times change?
> ▶ Who has custody of the children?
> ▶ What is the visitation schedule?
> ▶ Who pays related expenses for school (transportation, books, etc.) and unusual expenses (lessons, camp, braces, etc.)? What about college costs?
> ▶ Who will claim the children as dependents on their income tax forms?

Paying Tolls: What to Expect of Your Lawyer's Billing Process

First, let's put the billing process in perspective. Abraham Lincoln said, "A lawyer's time and advice are his stock and trade." That is, a lawyer has no goods on shelves to sell, only time and advice. Most people would never expect to walk into a store, take items to the cash register, and ask to be allowed to take the items out of the store without paying for them. But some people expect to be able to obtain legal advice without paying for it.

On the other hand, attorneys have the reputation for charging for full hours of time when only a few minutes are spent. So don't be afraid to ask for exact documentation: don't accept a simple invoice that merely states something like, "services rendered, three hours," with a sum of money due. You have no idea what the services were and how much time was spent. It is your money, so ask, ask, ask what you're paying for.

Get in writing how charges are allocated: phone time, copies, faxes, mailings, filing fees, court costs, bonding requirements, paralegals, expert witnesses, mileage charges, attorney time, and the time of other members of the firm. Charges can mushroom overnight. Fees will range all over the

Hazard!
Keep an Eye on the Meter

An important issue for hiring any professional is the cost—how much and how allocated (per flat hour, half hour, quarterly, fractions of time rounded up). You don't want surprises. Also, keep in mind that although many good lawyers are not comfortable talking about fees, this does not necessarily mean they are not honest. You may simply have to bring up the subject.

map, depending on the area in which you live. Obviously, New York and Beverly Hills will have a higher per-hour cost than Cedar Rapids, Iowa. The cost of living in your area is a factor, but so are your attorney's experience and overall results. It's a good idea to keep a phone log of incoming and outgoing calls (the ones you make) to your attorney. Note the subject and amount of time for the calls.

Again, *never, never, never* give an attorney carte blanche to run up enormous bills—many will. Sometimes attorneys can run up their bills to incredible proportions. They can do it in one of three ways:

1. They are often so busy coping with every deadline as each comes up, that they don't pay attention. Their meters don't get turned off because they are always scrambling and are not really organized.
2. Many don't understand the finances. When they look at an issue, they don't have the sense to say, "This is not my bailiwick. Let's talk to somebody who can tell you whether are looking at $5 or $50,000."
3. Some of them really and truly are deliberately goosing up their bills by being adversarial at every corner.

Most lawyers charge by the hour, and those who are in greater demand will usually charge more for their time. But price is not always a measure of skill. Find out the *range of fees* in your community for simple to more complex cases. Friends may discuss their experiences with you, but in shopping for a lawyer, inquire about fees and charges. If a lawyer you are considering charges substantially above or below the amount you have found, then find out why.

Another thing that you will find (not surprisingly) is that inexperienced lawyers charge less, unless they are really brazen. But it may take more time to finish the same work. Taking all things into consideration, if you can afford the more expensive lawyer who has a top-notch, well-earned reputation, you probably are better off using this lawyer. Many times that reputation may have a significant effect on the outcome of your case.

Retainer Fees. Most lawyers require you to put up a sum of money up front before they will take the case. This is called a "retainer fee," and it can run from a few hundred to several thousand dollars, depending on the expected problems with the case. State laws require that this money be deposited into a separate client trust account, not into the lawyer's regular bank account.

You need to understand clearly if the retainer is all or partially refundable. If the retainer is refundable, your lawyer likely will keep track of the time and charge against the deposit as the case progresses. If there is money left over, your lawyer will refund it to you. On the other hand, if the money is spent, additional retainer funds will be required from you.

However, keep in mind that the retainer is normally *not refundable* if you drop your case or find a new lawyer unless the retainer was very large and little work was done. This is because divorce filings are frequently withdrawn, and much effort can go into the initial work.

We strongly recommend some type of fee agreement. This protects the lawyer as well as you, the client. Go over the proposed fee agreement very carefully. If there is something in it that you do not like or understand, it is critical that you bring it into the open. For example, if there are payment requirements that you cannot make, ask if the provision can be changed.

Do not be angry if a lawyer cannot tell you precisely how much your case will cost. It is impossible to accurately predict all of the variables that may arise. For the same reason, you should be wary if a lawyer quotes a flat fee for a total package. If your case drags on, the lawyer will not be very mo-

---

Hazard!

Never Forget—You Are the Driver

Don't forget, your attorney works for you. Don't be afraid to take control. If you don't understand what is going on, ask. If you can't get a reasonable or clear explanation, shop for another attorney.

tivated to put in the extra hours that will be required for taking the case to completion.

There is another element in the expense of divorcing—court costs, the miscellaneous charges made by the court in connection with the processing of the case. They include administrative filing costs of pleadings and the cost to transcribe the record, if necessary. Finally, many other miscellaneous costs can be associated with a divorce: hiring an investigator; court-reporter charges for transcribing depositions; subpoena fees; process server fees; and costs for photocopying, postage, long-distance telephone calls, faxes, and the like.

On the Road with Your Attorney: How to Work Together Effectively

Once you've hired an attorney, there are several factors that are crucial to a successful working relationship.

Communicate Openly. As your case progresses, communication with your attorney and other advisers is critical. Your relationship with your lawyer is central when it comes to orchestrating the various issues within your divorce. We hope this relationship is positive and continues to improve as your case progresses. If your lawyer does not want to listen to your ideas, watch out: there will be trouble on the road ahead.

Be Open and Truthful. Another key ingredient in the relationship between a lawyer and client is that you, the client, should be open and candid with your lawyer. A relationship of trust and credibility is essential. Your lawyer needs to know the facts to develop a strategy and make any predictions about the outcome of the case.

Some clients lie or withhold information if they have done something really dumb. But often these are some of the most important details your lawyer needs to know. Everybody makes mistakes, and it is unlikely that an experienced lawyer will be shocked by anything you say.

If you lie about facts such as assets or income, the truth usually will come out, and your attorney will have lost credibility with your spouse's attorney. It can be disastrous if a judge finds out that you've lied. (If your lawyer suggests that you lie or keeps quiet while you continue deceiving the other side or the court, you have the wrong lawyer. A competent lawyer does not have to rely on such tactics.)

Besides violating ethical and legal standards, it is stupid to lie because your spouse usually will know what the truth is, and it will come out. Lies are gasoline on the fires of litigation. The old adage is true, "If you tell the truth, you will not have to worry that you forgot what you said."

Organize and Focus on What You Want to Accomplish. When you have an appointment, organize your thoughts, questions (write them down), and the information you are providing the lawyer. Have some specific goals in mind. This practice is better for you and your lawyer, and especially your pocketbook. This is one of the times to remember your lawyer is not your therapist or rent-a-friend.

Agree on How to Handle Phone Calls and Messages. You may need to call your lawyer rather than make an appointment for an office visit. During your initial interview, find out your lawyer's preference about telephone calls. Many lawyers, who have a hectic day, will return calls in the evening, so be sure and make it clear if you don't want the lawyer to call you at home or leave messages.

Busy lawyers generally do not block out time during the day to receive calls, so it is likely that you will have to leave a message and wait for your call to be returned. Before you call, think of a way to condense your question or information in case you need to leave a message. This can minimize the need for telephone tag. In addition, it may be that the secretary or paralegal can answer your question or obtain the information you need. This may save you money because the lawyer will bill for calls, whereas the secretary may not. And if the secretary does bill, it should be at a substantially lower rate.

Don't call a lawyer's home unless it is a true emergency that must be dealt with immediately. And if your problem is domestic violence, call 911, not your lawyer. Your lawyer is not going to come to your house and get in the middle of a confrontation. Most matters will have to wait until the next morning before they can be acted on anyway.

The telephone can turn into a source of irritation and conflict between a lawyer and client either because the client calls too often about unimportant matters or the lawyer seldom or never returns calls. If a problem develops, honestly consider whether you are the problem. Look at your log of calls. (You *are* keeping a phone log, aren't you?) If it's the lawyer's problem, find out, if you can, from the lawyer if this is normal practice, and, if there is something that can be done to make things go more efficiently. You need to know if this is the lawyer's style, or if your lawyer is avoiding you. You may need to sched-

Hazard!

Stay in Touch, but Not Too Much

Don't make a pest of yourself on the phone. If you will want to spend a long time on the phone every time there is call from the lawyer, you will be less likely to have your calls returned promptly. In contrast, if you're prudent with your phone calls, your lawyer may put you at the top of the callback list, because then your lawyer knows you're not going to waste time and the call will be quick.

ule an appointment to discuss this with the lawyer or write a letter stating your concerns. Sometimes a lawyer may not be aware of the situation. A good lawyer will want to know if there is a problem in your relationship.

Working with "the Pit Crew": Your Lawyer's Staff

Not only is it critical for you to have a good relationship with your attorney, it is equally critical to have a good relationship with your lawyer's receptionist, secretary, and/or paralegal staff. Paralegals have formal training and experience in legal matters, and many lawyers place great responsibility on them. In fact, it is customary for the administrative support staff to know more about some aspects of your case than your lawyer.

Have you ever thought about who keeps track of all the stuff? Don't count on the attorney—it's usually the staff! They will usually keep track of information about dates, court times, depositions, and office appointments. So save your contacts with your lawyer for more important issues.

Remember to treat the administrative staff with respect—not just because it is civil, but also it is in your best interests, too. If they conclude that you are easy to get along with, your case can get priority—maybe in scheduling appointments and in having your calls returned. They are usually the gatekeepers of the lawyer and have significant indirect power.

> *Don't ignore your lawyer's administrative support staff. Be nice to them; a thank-you note, flowers, or candy works wonders for these hardworking and often underappreciated cogs in the wheel of a good law office.*

▶ Route 2: Choosing Mediation or Arbitration

Going to battle is definitely not the only way to resolve the issues that are guaranteed to arise during your divorce. If an attorney tells you that the only place your divorce can be settled is in the courtroom, ask him or her about mediation and arbitration, and if he or she isn't a fan of these strategies you might want to bid a quick goodbye. You are dealing with someone who is not tuned in to the possibility of mediation, arbitration, negotiation, or even a friendly parting of you and your spouse.

Before entering into mediation or arbitration, you need to know the difference between them. In arbitration and mediation, a neutral third party is used. But this is where the similarities end. Here are some of the differences:

▶ In *arbitration,* both husband and wife agree to give the arbitrator the power to decide the dispute as a judge would. There are two types:

  1. In *binding arbitration,* you agree beforehand to abide by the decision as if it were law.
  2. In *straight arbitration,* if you don't like it, you can go elsewhere.

▶ The purpose of *mediation* is for both husband and wife to come to a mutually acceptable settlement. The mediator does no individual counseling and is limited to gathering data, setting the ground rules, and keeping both parties on track. Throughout mediation, alternative solutions are offered, issues are clarified, and a settlement is arrived at. If you and your spouse are communicating, then you should consider exploring the mediation route.

A Mediation Case Study

Elizabeth chose to go into mediation, but only after she went attorney shopping. She interviewed eight different attorneys over a variety of issues. When she told one of them about her husband's temper, she was advised to get an injunction immediately. That way, if Harold became threatening or harassing, she could throw him out. By law, he would have three days to respond. The thought of it made her extremely upset. There had never been any physical abuse, it was more along the lines of yelling, shouting, and stomping around the house. She didn't like the idea of throwing him on the street.

To her dismay, she discovered that the $3,000 retainer fee that this attorney requested would merely cover the cost of filing for the injunction. Her divorce would cost much, much more. The total marital assets she was looking at amounted to $200,000, mostly from the family residence. She called a friend of hers, a divorce attorney in another state, for advice and a reality check.

The divorce attorney countered what the first attorney had said, adding, "An injunction is merely a piece of paper that says you aren't to do anything that is harmful. Most times, it is plain B.S. If someone has his socks knocked off with such an order, it will incite him to actually be violent, even if he ordinarily wouldn't be violent. Throwing someone out of the house will create a negative mode and will make mediating the dissolution even tougher. If you do not feel that you or your children are physically threatened, do not get an injunction."

One Way to Go: Mediation as a Choice

Mediation doesn't eliminate your need for a competent attorney. But it does require voluntary participation of both husband and wife.

Mediators can be retired or active family law commissioners or judges, a lawyer who is skilled in family law, or a lawyer who is skilled in family law and has some counseling background. Mediators can also be psychologists or other professionals who have been trained in mediation.

Many people may believe that one of the objectives of mediation is to attempt to get couples through the divorce process with the least amount of pain. However, you should keep in mind that mediation is sometimes more painful than divorce because you and your spouse will face each other directly.

Also, be aware that many lawyers aren't great proponents of mediation, because it costs a fraction of the settlement costs. The lawyer would charge on an hourly basis and it usually takes from 4 to 10 sessions for couples to go through the whole process. However, the best divorce lawyers have no problems when their clients participate in mediation. In fact, they actually encourage their clients to do it. They know how to support their clients as they go through the process and chip in with their advice when the clients come back with questions.

This is not to say that attorneys have no place in mediation; in fact, the contrary is true. A good lawyer will help you guard against one of the dangers of mediation—inappropriate valuation of property. They fear that this more informal approach could miss or inappropriately value properties that are divided in the marital settlement. Before you sign any agreements that come out of mediation, always have them reviewed to determine whether they represent your best interests.

The bottom line is that no single person has all the answers. Some type of compromise may well be the only solution. There are usually two key similarities among cases of those who achieved successful divorces (i.e., they came away with their self-esteem intact and a reasonable or acceptable property settlement): They had a *nonadversarial attorney* representing each side, and they kept the channels of *communication open.*

On the Road via Mediation: How to Make It Work

Obviously, the selection of the mediator is critical if this process is to be given a chance to work. An experienced divorce lawyer—this is another time when experience counts—in a metropolitan area will know a variety of mediators with varying backgrounds and strengths. Get recommendations from your lawyer before you turn to other sources.

You may be thinking, "I bet my lawyer does not want the mediation to work because if we cannot settle, the lawyer would make a lot more money." Again, the better lawyers would be pleased to see their clients avoid the trauma of a contested divorce. These top-notch lawyers want what is best for their clients. All lawyers have fiduciary obligation to their clients—that means that they must always put their clients' best interests first.

Mediators come from different professions: mental health, financial planning, law, or social work. Most important, however, the person must have training in mediation and be knowledgeable about issues confronted in a divorce.

You'll also want to focus on the mediator's style, and decide which will work best for your situation. Some will simply be a third party to facilitate communications as you and your spouse sort through issues. Others will provide advice about particular issues, such as child custody or property division. And still others will assist you and your spouse in working through some of the emotional issues of divorce.

A goal of the mediation process is to draft the outline of a settlement. You and your spouse will then have an attorney take the outline and prepare a formal separation agreement based on the terms of the mediation. If you are using only your spouse's lawyer, seek a second opinion from your own lawyer. Have this lawyer explain the pros and cons and significance of each provision. Remember, you will have to live with this the rest of your life!

An Alternate Route: Arbitration Instead of Mediation

Arbitration is another way to avoid lengthy and expensive litigation. An arbitrator acts as your own private judge who conducts a "mini-trial" of sorts, in which the parties and their attorneys present their cases. Arbitration is used more in some areas than in others, and can be particularly attractive if you live in an area with a huge backlog of cases. If you agree in advance to what is called *binding arbitration,* the arbitrator's decisions are final and become a court order just as if you had gone before a judge. On the other hand, you can agree that the decision of the arbitrator is only *advisory,* in which case you would not be required to follow their decision.

▶ Route 3: Driving Solo, via a Do-it-Yourself Divorce

As mentioned at the beginning of this chapter, the do-it-yourself approach to divorce is *not recommended.* Many people going through a divorce may be thinking, "This is just too complicated and scary. I think my spouse and I should do our own divorce." We suggest you think again, because there have been many "do-it-yourself" cases where one person was secretly working with a lawyer and getting advice on how to take advantage of the unrepresented spouse.

Know Before You Go: Six Mistakes Typically Made by Do-It-Yourselfers

The following paragraphs describe six types of mistakes made by couples who are trying to be *honest and open* in a do-it-yourself divorce. Imagine the mistakes that could be made if one spouse (or both) were shrewd and dishonest!

Hazard!
The Rules of the Arbitration Road

▶ Be sure you understand whether the arbitrator's decision will be *binding* or only *advisory*.

▶ There is no attorney-client privilege with a mediator, arbitrator, or special master, so anything you say could come out in court.

▶ An arbitrator can be used for the entire divorce process or only to resolve certain issues. The arbitrator may even offer a combination approach, mediating initially, but making a decision for you if you cannot agree.

▶ Shop for an arbitrator in the same way as you would for a mediator, but you will find that it is rare that an arbitrator is not a lawyer. Retired judges frequently open arbitration practices. If this is something you want to consider, ask your lawyer to recommend some good arbitrators.

▶ In some jurisdictions the court, upon request, will approve a lawyer to act as what is called a "special master" to get past a problem area. This appointed lawyer usually will have a particular area of expertise, such as the division of pensions (a topic discussed in detail in Chapter 3). Again, your attorney should play a significant role in deciding whether to use a special master and who that person should be.

▶ When divorcing couples gear up for a courtroom encounter, it's rare for both sides to come out of the courtroom content with the aftermath of a divorce. So if you feel you may be caught up in someone else's agenda—yes, attorneys sometimes *do not* act in your best interest—strongly consider getting a second opinion and input from one of the experts identified in this chapter.

Problems with Income Taxes. If you do not understand the tax consequences of the transfer of certain property, such as a house, you may be stuck with a huge tax bill.

Forgotten and Missed Assets. If you don't understand what constitutes marital property, some property may be mistakenly transferred, such as inherited property that has been kept in your own name.

Mistakes with Pensions. In many cases, the retirement accounts are the most valuable marital asset, so mistakes in this area can be very costly. Spouses who do not fully understand their own retirement plans could grossly undervalue what is to be divided. Some also fail to understand the consequences of the death of the nonemployee. In many cases, the nonemployee died, and the company ended up with that person's share of the pension. This means that your heirs would get none of your share of the pension!

Omissions in the Settlement Agreement. Drafting a comprehensive agreement can be a real challenge. For example, a couple with children may leave out some of the major points of their understanding about visitation rights. They could forget to state who will be responsible for some major credit card debts and underestimate the amount of child support that the noncustodial parent owes.

Inappropriate Selection of the State in which to Get Divorced. Consider this example: One couple had separated because of the husband's abuse, and the wife left the state. Several years later, the husband called the wife to see if they could agree on a divorce. One of the topics discussed was whether to file the action in the state where the wife lived or in the state where the husband lived. They agreed to a divorce in the state where the husband lived. In that state, the property rights of the spouses end when they separate, but in the state where the wife now lived, the property rights continue right up to the time of the divorce. Therefore, although she was a victim of serious abuse, the wife lost the opportunity to have a larger portion of her ex-husband's pension plan.

Inattention to Post-Decree Matters. The details of completing the final paperwork are often put aside for another day. Some couples don't understand how to transfer some real estate in another state, taking months to get things straightened out. Some couples never prepare their final orders—and they typically won't find out for many months that they're still married!

▶ Determining Your Route

Legal matters can be overwhelming and confusing. Shakespeare wrote, "The first thing we do, let's kill all the lawyers." We know that there will be times when you would gladly eliminate your attorney. It's not a fun thing you are going through, and they often bear the brunt of all that ails you.

But the reality is that unless your situation is so uncomplicated—for example, you don't have kids and you have little or no assets—you need a good attorney on your team. The information we have given you in this chapter should ease your way through this legal maze.

You Take the High Road

Divvying up the House and Everything in It

On the long road to getting divorced, there are many financial issues you need to consider and decide with your soon-to-be-ex-spouse. Let's start with how to divide your property.

▶ Getting Started: Map Your Route

What do you think about when you think of property? Your joint savings account? The house you jointly own or that is in your spouse's name, even though you've paid for half of it? You may think you already know all about property. But do your views meet the legal tests of what property is? Therefore, when looking at the property issues in divorce, couples usually ask these four questions:

1. What constitutes property?
2. What is it worth and how is that value determined?
3. At what date will it be valued?
4. How will it be divided?

The next sections of this chapter answer these questions and show how to protect what belongs to you, focusing on your house and other physical assets. These answers are your first stops on the road to post-divorce financial security. In Chapter 3 we'll cover your (and your spouse's) pensions, IRAs, and other retirement plans.

Stop #1: What Constitutes "Property"?

Property includes such assets as your family home, rental property, cars, jewelry, and art or antique collections. It can also include your bank accounts, mutual funds, stocks and bonds, cash value life insurance, IRAs, and retirement plans. And yes, it covers career assets and "PHTS" or "PWTS" (putting your husband or wife through school, which we'll discuss later in this chapter). As you can see, there is virtually no limit to what can be considered property.

Laws about division of property vary from state to state. Property issues account for a large number of appeals! Although there are exceptions to just about everything, when it comes to property, it is usually divided into two categories: separate and marital.

In general, *separate property* is property that will not be divided, and it includes what you and your spouse brought into your marriage, inherited during your marriage, or received as a gift during your marriage.

On the other hand, *marital property* can be divided, and it includes everything acquired during your marriage, no matter whose name it's in. In some states, marital property also includes the increase in value of your (and your spouse's) separate property.

Do you know what kind of state you live in and what rules of property division your state follows? There are three different types of states:

1. In *community property* states (Arizona, California, Idaho, Louisiana, Nevada, New Mexico, Texas, Washington, and Wisconsin), property that is not subject to division of the court—that is, your and your spouse's *separate* property—needs to be identified first. The court may then decide on how your *marital,* or *community,* property is divided. Some community property states require that all property acquired during your marriage be split equally, whereas others divvy up assets in the same way as equitable distribution states do.

2. *Equitable distribution* states usually agree that your marital property be divided equitably, or fairly, between you and your spouse.

3. Finally, in *equal distribution* states, the property is divided—you guessed it—equally.

Once you know how your state handles property division, you can decide which property is yours or your spouse's, and which is owned jointly. The great majority of states have detailed statutes that categorize property. Your attorney will be able to tell you how property is divided in your state.

Stop #2: How Much Is Your Property Worth?

To explain how to determine the value of your property, let's look at some examples.

Example #1: The Interest on a Savings Account. Beth and her husband are getting a divorce. When Beth got married, she had $1,000 in a savings account. During the marriage, her $1,000 earned $100 in interest. Her account is now worth $1,100. She did not add her husband's name to the account when they married.

Her property is $1,000, because she kept it in her name only. In some states, the $100 in interest goes into the pot of marital assets to be divided, because that is the increase in value of her separate property. On the other hand, if Beth had put her husband's name on the account, she would have turned the entire account into a marital asset. In essence, she would have made a gift to the marriage.

Example #2: The Changing Value of a House. In some marriages, frequently with second or third marriages, both people may bring real estate into the marriage. Suppose that Beth owned a house when she got married, which she kept in her name only. At that time, the house was worth $100,000 and had a mortgage on it of $70,000, so the equity was $30,000. Now Beth is getting divorced. Today the house is worth $150,000. The mortgage is down to about $50,000. Equity has increased to $100,000.

	AT MARRIAGE	AT DIVORCE
Value	$100,000	$150,000
Mortgage	− 70,000	− 50,000
Equity	$ 30,000	$100,000

These numbers lead to only one conclusion in the valuation of property: the increase in value is the increase in the total equity, or $70,000.

Example #3: A House that's Jointly Owned. Let's reverse the situation. Suppose Beth put her husband's name on the deed to the house when they got married. After all, they were going to be together for the rest of their lives, right? As soon as Beth put her husband's name on the deed, the house was turned into a marital asset. She gave what is called a presumptive gift to the marriage.

Example #4: The Changing Value of Stock. What if Beth owned stock worth $10,000 when she got married? On the day of the divorce, it is worth $9,000. Is that a $1,000 marital loss? Yes. If there is a marital increase on one asset, it can be offset with a marital loss. If Beth had owned a house and it had decreased in value, the same would apply.

Example #5: What Is Jewelry Worth? Assume that when Beth got married, her husband gave her an eight-carat diamond ring. Let's suppose they're now in court and she is testifying that the ring was a gift from her husband, so it is her personal property. He says, "Are you kidding? I would not *give* you an eight-carat diamond. That was an investment, therefore it is marital property."

The judge decides. Typically, however (or stereotypically), women get to keep their jewelry, their furs, and similar types of gifts. Men get to keep their tools, their guns, and their golf clubs.

Example #6: The Value of Artwork, Antiques, or Collectibles. What if Beth's husband had given her an $80,000 painting for her birthday? She claimed it was a gift, and he claimed it was an investment and therefore should be treated as marital property.

In this case, the judge called it an investment. Because it was not the type of thing that most people would freely give as a gift, it was seen as an investment for the family and that is why it was considered marital property. But remember, you can never predict what the judge will decide!

What happens when both parties want the same item? Let's say Beth and her husband had divided all their property except for one item. They couldn't agree who was going to get the set of antique crystal that had come from England.

Reason and logic are needed here. Negotiation skills come into play, along with a need to prioritize what is wanted, along with the value of the item. We know that *emotional value* is a factor, but it can't be measured. When both spouses want the same item, obtaining an item can become an out-of-control quest. There have been cases where the item may have originally cost a few thousand dollars, and the couple spends megathousands trying to "win" it in the courtroom. Instead of spending the money for attorneys, Beth and her husband could take the savings and return to England to buy a new set!

Example #7: The Value of Home Furnishings. When it comes to home furnishings, most values are fairly low. Home furnishings aren't usually included on the list of assets, because couples just divide them up. If they are to be valued, the typical value is what you can get from a garage sale.

Stop #3: When Will Your Property Be Valued?

How do you decide the end date of accrual of marital property? The day you decided to separate? The day you started living separately? Or, the day when your marriage is finally dissolved either in court or through mediation or arbitration? The rules vary from state to state. For example, some would value the property on the date you and your spouse physically separated, whereas others would continue until the final divorce decree is granted. Don't assume anything; check with your attorney about the rules in your state.

Stop #4: How Your Property Will Be Divided—A Case Study

Dividing property almost always takes some finesse. It's not as simple as taking the total value of your marital assets and just divvying them up. Emotions, perceived value, even not wanting your spouse to have something because, well—just *because*—it all plays a part.

Let's look at an example of how a case can play out. Marilyn and Tom Baxter have been married for 35 years. She's a homemaker caring for their four kids and has not worked outside of their home for pay. Tom earns $150,000 per year and has started a business in the basement of their home. He expects the new business to create revenues after he retires. Their home is worth $135,000 and is mortgage free. His pension is valued at $90,000. Their joint savings is $28,000. Tom estimates his basement business is worth $75,000. Their combined assets total $328,000. If you assume a 50-50 property split, each would receive $164,000.

Here are the Baxters' assets at the time of their divorce:

House	$135,000
Pension	90,000
Savings	28,000
Business	75,000
Total	$328,000

Splitting the property and assets down the middle is often not the most equitable division. In this scenario, Marilyn wants the house. The value of the house will remain in her column on a typical property settlement worksheet. Tom wants what most men want in the distribution of assets: the pension. We'll put the pension in his column.

Tom also has some other thoughts. With the demands of his growing basement business, he needs cash. He wants the $28,000 savings account. Add the savings account to his column. Because Tom feels the business in the basement is his, he wants it all as his property. Put the business in his column.

The division now looks like this:

	ASSETS	MARILYN	TOM
House	$135,000	$135,000	—
Pension	90,000	—	90,000
Savings	28,000	—	28,000
Business	75,000	—	75,000
Total	$328,000	$135,000	$193,000

Her assets total $135,000 and his assets total $193,000. If we were to look at a 50-50 property split, he would owe her $29,000. Although Tom has a large income of $150,000 a year, he does not want to give up any of the business or pension or savings.

Using a Property Settlement Note. We could even out this division with a property settlement note. Tom could pay Marilyn $29,000 over time, like a note at the bank. He can make monthly payments with current market interest. Or, he may be able to borrow funds directly from the bank, because he has assets, including a savings account comparable to what he would owe.

A *property settlement note* is an agreement to pay a specified amount for an agreed-upon length of time with reasonable interest. It is still considered division of property, so the payer cannot deduct it from taxable income. The payee does not pay taxes on the principal—only on the interest. It is important to collateralize this note, meaning that the payer should pledge something of value to guarantee it, in case the payer doesn't pay on the note.

If no other asset is available, it is possible to collateralize this note with a qualified pension by using a Qualified Domestic Relations Order (QDRO), a legal document that directs the administrator of a pension plan as to what amount (either percentage or dollar amount) is to be given to a nonemployee spouse. If the payer defaults on the payments of a property settlement note, then the payee can collect pursuant to the terms of the QDRO agreement from the pension. A QDRO can be used to collaterialize a property settlement note.

Suppose Marilyn does not like the settlement suggested. She believes she is owed the house and wants half of her husband's pension because, in their 35 years of marriage, she helped him earn his pension by caring for their children and managing their household. She also wants half of the savings, because she doesn't want to be left without any cash. But she agrees that the basement business is Tom's.

So let's adjust the columns, keeping the house in Marilyn's column; splitting the pension, putting $45,000 in each column; dividing the savings, placing $14,000 in both columns; and crediting Tom with the business.

The property split now looks like this:

	ASSETS	MARILYN	TOM
House	$135,000	$135,000	—
Pension	90,000	45,000	45,000
Savings	28,000	14,000	14,000
Business	75,000	—	75,000
Total	$328,000	$194,000	$134,000

Marilyn's assets are now valued at $194,000 and Tom's at $134,000. Marilyn now owes Tom $30,000 to make a 50-50 property settlement. But it's not that simple. She does not have a job and has limited skills. It is unlikely she would be able to get a job that pays her a high income.

Her largest asset is the house, which is not a liquid asset. And there are ongoing expenses to maintaining the house. It's paid for, but it doesn't create revenues to help her buy groceries. She could rent out rooms for additional income, but that rarely works and it creates a lifestyle that she may not want. How is she going to pay this $30,000 to Tom? The prospects are bleak. Given that Marilyn is in her mid-50s, has never worked outside the home, and her largest asset is not liquid, this unequal division may be considered the most equitable.

Awarding alimony comes after the property is divided. The reason for this is that alimony can be based on the amount of property received, so it is important to look first at the property division. (Alimony is discussed in Chapter 4.)

▶ The Fork in the Road: Equal vs. Equitable Division of Property

In property division, couples need to trade assets back and forth until they agree on the division. In an equitable property division state, you split the property equitably. It does not mean *equal;* it means *fair.*

On the other hand, the word *equality* suggests fairness and equity for all parties involved. Unfortunately, the required equal division of property in some states has forced more sales of family assets, especially the family home, so that the proceeds can be divided between spouses. The net result is increased dislocation and disruption, especially in the lives of minor children, if any. This is not fair, in that the needs and interests of the children are not considered in many cases.

A second problem of equality is that a 50-50 division of your property may not produce equal results—or equal standards of living after the divorce —if you and your spouse are unequally situated at the time of divorce. This is most evident in the situation of the older homemaker, as seen in the example of Marilyn Baxter. After a marital life devoted to homemaking, she is typically without substantial skills and experience in the workplace. Most likely, she will require a greater share of the property to cushion the income loss she suffers at divorce. Rarely is she in an equal economic position at divorce.

Generally, a 50-50 division is started when property is divided in an equitable division state. A major consideration can be how much separate property you have. Let's say your spouse has $2 million in separate property. Your marital estate totals $200,000. A judge who knows your spouse has $2 million worth of separate property may not give your spouse 50 percent of the marital property. Instead, the judge's attitude may be, "Well, you have $2 million in separate property, so you get none of the marital property."

▶ Three Possible Routes for "Dividing" The House

Most assets are in houses and pensions. How you get your share out of either creates some anxiety, and tension is in the air. There are three basic options to approaching the issue of who gets the house. You can sell the house, buy out your spouse's half, or continue to own the property jointly after the divorce. Let's look more closely at each route.

Route 1: Sell the House and Split the Proceeds

Selling the house and dividing the profits that remain after sales costs and the mortgage is paid off is the easiest and "cleanest" way of dividing equity. However, you'll still need to address these concerns:

▶ the basis and possible capital gains (addressed later in this chapter),
▶ buying another house versus renting, and
▶ being able to qualify for a new loan.

Route 2: One Spouse Buys Out the Other

Another way to "divide" the house is for one of you to buy out the other's half. This approach works if one of you wants to remain in the house or wants to own the house. But there are difficulties with this option that need to be considered.

First of all, you need to agree on a value of the property. For purposes of the divorce, value is the equity in the house.

Next, decide on the dollar amount of the buyout. Will the dollar amount have subtracted from it selling costs and capital gains taxes (if any)?

Then you and your spouse need to agree on a method of payment. If payments will be made over a specified period, the terms need to be comfortable for both parties. The payment could be as simple as giving up another marital asset in trade for the equity in the house. The house could be refinanced to withdraw cash to pay the other spouse, or a note payable can be drawn up with terms of payment that are agreeable to both parties. Reasonable interest should be attached to the note, and it should be collateralized with a deed of trust on the property. One problem with this arrangement is that it keeps you in a debtor-creditor relationship with your ex.

There is another problem with buying out your spouse's half. Let's say you get the house and both names are on the deed. Your ex can *quitclaim* the deed to you so that only your name is on the deed. Now, you can sell it whenever you want. Although your ex's name comes off the deed, it remains on the mortgage. What happens if you don't pay the mortgage? The mortgage company will come to your ex for payment. It doesn't care that you are divorced. The only way to remove your ex's name from the mortgage is to assume the loan in your name *if* your mortgage is assumable.

Route 3: Share Ownership of the House, Jointly

The other option—continuing to own the property jointly—is often used when a couple wants their kids to stay in the house until the children finish school or reach a certain age, or until the resident ex-spouse remarries or cohabits. You and your spouse agree to sell the house after the kids have graduated from school and split the proceeds evenly. Whoever stays in the house in the meantime can pay the mortgage payment, while all other costs of maintaining the house plus taxes and repairs are split evenly. Again, this continues a tie between the two of you that may create stress.

Rubbernecking: Check Out How These Couples Divided their Houses

Here are some examples to help put all these options into perspective.

Scenario #1. Mark and Susan had very good jobs when they decided to divorce in 1986. Susan wanted to stay in the house with the three children and buy out Mark's half of the house with a property settlement note. Interest rates were high. The note was drawn with her agreeing to pay Mark his half of the equity at 14 percent interest. Then property values began to decline. Susan's half of the equity was losing value, while Mark's was earning 14 percent, even after the interest rates plummeted.

At the time they drew up this agreement, no one presumed that interest rates or property values would go down. It is always a risk when you make agreements that extend out into the future. These risks run both ways.

Scenario #2. In contrast, Lila and Keith had divided all their property, with her owing him $5,000. She kept the house and was going to sell it in three years when their daughter was out of high school. The house had $20,000 of equity in it at the time of divorce. They both agreed that when she sold the house in three years, she would give him his $5,000. Lila's attorney knew Susan's lawyer and had heard about the case where Susan was paying 14 percent interest. Lila's attorney suggested, "Because $5,000 represents 25 percent of the equity, why don't you agree on a percentage? That way, when you sell the house you give him 25 percent of the profits. If the house declines in value and you only get $10,000 profit, you are not paying him half. Or if it goes up, you both win because you both get more."

Therefore, if you are considering dividing assets beyond one year of your divorce, it's recommended that you discuss with your attorney negotiating a *percentage* rather than an exact *dollar amount.*

Scenario #3. The previous scenarios have featured women who were more attached to their homes than their husbands, as is usually presumed to be the case. But should a woman always negotiate to keep the home? Not necessarily. There are cases when the wife should not keep the house. Consider Bob and Cindy. Cindy is 32 years old and Bob is 33. They have been married 12 years. They have two kids, nine and five years old. Cindy is the custodial parent.

Cindy needs three more years to finish college and get her degree and another year to earn her teaching credential. She estimates that she will earn $33,000 a year as a new teacher. Between going to school and caring for the kids, she will not be able to earn income. Bob is offering to help Cindy through school by paying maintenance of $2,400 per month for one year, then $1,500 per month for two additional years.

Cindy's expenses with the two kids are $3,000 per month. This includes her expenses for school, which average $350 per month. Bob earns $75,000 per year and brings home $57,570 per year after taxes. His expenses are $2,000 per month. Cindy and Bob had trouble staying within their budget while they were married. Cindy loved to shop and tended to overspend, maxing their credit cards to their limits.

The family home has a fair market value of $220,000 with a mortgage of $125,000. Monthly payments are $1,500 per month, including real estate taxes. Cindy wants to remain in the house with the kids.

But it doesn't make economic sense for Cindy to keep a house with a $1,500 monthly payment when she has no income of her own and is relying on maintenance to make that payment for her. She could rent a smaller house close to where she currently lives for $750 to $800 per month.

She will receive some type of alimony for a few years, as well as child support for the kids. Selling the house will release cash that in turn can create income to supplement the alimony and child support she will receive until she gets her teaching credential.

Plus, she can't count on maintenance that Bob has agreed to pay on the house, because what if Bob loses his job? Both Cindy and Bob need counseling on cash flow and budgeting. Both must understand that whatever scenario they follow, it will have a major impact on their financial, emotional, parenting, and relationship lives. You may need to consider some of these issues as well (Chapters 5 and 6 can help you with future financial planning).

"Kicking the Tires": Assessing the Value of Your House

Whichever route you choose with respect to your house, you need to know what it's worth. If your spouse gets an appraisal, you should get one too. You can then agree to use one or the other, compromise between the two evaluations, or have the court decide.

An appraiser will work up an appraisal based on comparable properties that have sold within the past year and on current construction costs. Real estate appraisers are certified to work in specific areas, such as residential, commercial, or agricultural. Fees are usually $300 to $600, depending on the size of your property and its location.

Some people use a local real estate agent to get an estimate of their home's value. Real estate agents will often bring several agents in to preview your home and assess its value to potential buyers. After all, there is a listing possibility, so helping you now may earn them big bucks down the road. That's why there is no charge. If you go this route, ask for two listing figures—the first for a regular sale that could take several months and the other for a quick sale. You can call your local Board of Realtors® and ask for the average sale period in your area and price range to help guide you.

▶ Toll Road: Tax Considerations of Selling Your House

The Taxpayer Relief Act of 1997 created a big tax boon to the majority of taxpayers and is a disaster to others, in terms of capital gains. (*Capital gains* are the amount of profit you make when comparing the *adjusted basis* with the selling price of your last home. The *basis* is the original investment in your first home, increased by selling costs and any improvements.) But the 1997 law also created some complications. The details of the tax law are anything but simple, so let's travel down this road a bit to understand it better.

When selling your home at a profit, gains of up to $250,000 per person ($500,000 for married couples filing jointly) are still tax-free, if you have lived in your principal residence at least two of the last five years. If you lived there less than two years, you may still be able to claim some portion of the exclusion if you were forced to sell because of a change in the location of your employment, a health condition, or some other unforeseen circumstance. In that event, you would get only part of the $250,000 per person exclusion. And, the icing on the cake is that you can use this same exemption again after living in another home for at least two years of the last five.

The 1997 tax law also provides fulfillment of the residency requirement by the nonresident spouse. In other words, if you get the house in the divorce, sell it four years later, and split the profits with your ex, you each get to take the $250,000 exclusion because one of you fulfilled the residency requirement. Let's look at some examples.

John and Mary are getting divorced. John is awarded the jointly owned family home for four years. At the end of four years, John sells the home and 50 percent of the proceeds are sent to Mary.

Scenario A: John sells the house for $400,000. Mary will receive $200,000 and will be entitled to use her $250,000 exclusion, even though she has not lived in the house for the previous four years.

Scenario B: John sells the house for $750,000. Mary will receive $375,000. If the basis in the property was $100,000, Mary's portion of the basis is $50,000, leaving her with a $325,000 gain. Even though she uses her $250,000 exclusion, she will be taxed on $75,000 of gain.

Sales price	$750,000	Sales Price	$750,000
Basis	−100,000	John's Half	−375,000
Capital gain	$650,000	Mary's Half	$375,000
Mary's half of sales price			$375,000
Mary's half of basis			−50,000
Mary's half of capital gain			$325,000
Mary's exclusion			−250,000
Amount on which Mary will be taxed			$ 75,000

There is a situation in which you can be hit with a major tax bill, and that is if your home has appreciated beyond the amount of the exemption. Here's how:

Vicki and Stan are getting divorced and Vicki is taking the house, worth $750,000. The basis in the house is $200,000. Vicki decides to move to another city and buy another house for $750,000. She wants to maintain her current lifestyle and, as often happens, does not check into tax law or get financial advice before making a decision that may haunt her at a later time.

Her gain on the sale is $550,000. She will be able to use her $250,000 exclusion but will still have to pay taxes on the gain of $300,000, even though she bought another house of equal value!

Sales price	$750,000
Basis	−200,000
Capital gain	$550,000
Exclusion	−250,000
Amount on which Vicki will be taxed	$300,000

▶ At a Crossroads: Divvying Up Your Stuff

If you or your spouse is a pack rat, you may be sitting on a gold mine of goodies. Some are highly visible, whereas others may be buried in boxes and forgotten. According to a study done a few years ago by Foote, Cone and Belding, an advertising agency, 20 percent of all Americans collect things. Men lean toward coins, cars, and stamps, whereas women are more interested in antiques, gemstones, and books.

Do you have a valued collection of toys or old radios? How about stamps or buttons? Old beer cans? License plates? Does anyone in your household collect figurines—for example, some people collect Hummel figurines—which can be worth thousands of dollars?

What kind of collector are you? Better yet, what kind of collector is your spouse? The things that are accumulating that you thought were junk may indeed have significant value, especially now.

You want to get a valuation if you are going to keep the items, based on what you would receive in a sale on the open market within a fairly short period of time. If your spouse is going to take them, then you want the appraisal at top dollar. If you leave it up to the court, you may be in for a big surprise. Many courts will accept the "garage sale" value—great news if you are trying to get something at bargain prices; not so great if you are trying to trade assets worth a lot.

For antique buffs, the best time to get those items evaluated is during a time of inflation. Traditionally, they decline in value when deflation is in effect. On the other hand, if it's something that you love and you are in a period that is more deflationary, by all means, it is worth your while to get another appraisal. An important thing to keep in mind is that there are different kinds of appraisals. There is an insurance replacement appraisal and there is a market value appraisal.

Roadmap 2.1 represents only a partial list of what you need to consider when divvying up your stuff. Anything can be classed as a collectible if you have enough of them. There are books and clubs throughout the country that track values and trading sources. Use them as a valuable reference guide. Check with your local library for one near you. Also check out eBay. Note that a lot of these things are not huge and are easily portable. That means that they can freely exit the house—so be careful!

Roadmap 2.1

List of Collectibles to Consider and Appraise When Dividing Assets

Antiques (Furniture, carpets, fountain pens, banknotes, dolls, hat pins, stock certificates, toys, cookie cutters, kitchenware, china, glassware, games, currency, linens, and quilts)

Beer cans

Bottles

Bubblegum cards

Cameras

Cards (baseball, children's games, playing)

Cartoons

Catalogs

Ceramics

Clocks

Coins

Comics

Dolls (Shirley Temple, Storybook, Barbie, Beanie Babies)

Drawings

Election memorabilia

Elvis memorabilia

First editions and rare books

Figurines

Gems

Guns

Jukeboxes

License plates

Magazines

Movie memorabilia

Music boxes

Newspapers

Photographs

Pinball machines

Pipes

Plates

Political memorabilia

Postcards

Posters

Radios

Records

Science fiction books

Slot machines

Stamps

Tickets to historic events

Toys (all types)

Trains

War memorabilia

Watches

Also, keep in mind that gold coins, stamps, diamonds, and gems may be stashed in a safe-deposit box. These could be a source of cash for you, or at least a negotiating tool. Make sure you take pictures of the contents, even if you don't remove anything.

Be on the lookout for any hidden accounts. Although most people don't have secret bank accounts in foreign countries, this is always a possibility, especially if your spouse deals with large sums of cash, travels a great deal, and is thought of as being wealthy or well-to-do.

A variety of professionals other than attorneys and accountants can help you determine the value of your marital assets. Don't forget professional organizations and how-to books. Find appraisers, handymen, or others who can help. The Yellow Pages and ad sections of your newspaper always include service people in specific areas, and believe it or not, they usually can give you a good thumbnail appraisal of what your car, antiques, or that odd collection in the back of the garage is worth. If you have real works of art, a museum curator or art dealer could become your right hand.

All it takes to discover buried treasure is focused attention. Primarily, yours.

▶ On the Road to Work: What's a Career Worth?

With many couples, one spouse may have more significant assets tied to the career. These career assets include insurance (life, health, disability); vacation and sick pay; Social Security and unemployment benefits; stock options; and pension and retirement plans. Future promotions, job experience, seniority, professional contacts, and education are also considered career assets. In many cases, career assets should be considered in arriving at an equitable settlement.

In 1998, a highly publicized battle over career assets made the cover of *Fortune* magazine. Lorna and Gary Wendt were married for 32 years. He was the CEO of GE Capital; she a "corporate wife." At the time of the divorce, he declared the marital estate to be worth $21 million and offered her $8 million as her share. She balked, saying that the estate was worth $100 million. Her counter to him was that she wanted $50 million—half.

Lorna Wendt's position was that her husband's future pension benefits and stock options had been earned during their marriage. She argued that her contribution as the homemaker and later, wife of the CEO, enabled him to rise through the ranks to the top of an international organization. Her husband didn't agree.

In the early years of their marriage, she worked to support them while he attended Harvard Business School. They moved often while she handled the details of the household and took care of him and their two children. When he became CEO, she was expected to entertain often and extravagantly as his position required. She felt she was a 50-50 partner in the marriage and the accumulation of all assets.

The Wendt case broke through the long-held belief that "enough is enough"—that a spouse deserved enough to maintain her lifestyle—nothing more. In a landmark decision, the judge awarded her $20 million—far less than the $50 million she had requested, but far more than the $8 million her husband initially offered.

Even for couples who both work and both have careers, the assets tied to each of your careers probably will not be equal, so you and your spouse need to consider this inequality when dividing up your property.

▶ On the Road to School: Putting Your Husband or Wife through College

Consider the example of a family of simpler means, in which the husband is the dominant wage earner. It is not unusual for the wife to put the husband through school or help him become established while abandoning or postponing her own education. She may have quit her job to move from job to job with him.

Together, they made the decision to spend the time and energy to build his career with the expectation that she would share in the fruits of her investment through her husband's enhanced earning power. Over time, he has built up career assets, which are part of what he earns, even though they may not be paid out directly to him.

Even in two-income families, one spouse's career often takes priority over the other. Both spouses expect to share the rewards of that decision—at least, in the beginning of their marriage.

Some states even place a value on degrees such as the medical degree, the dental degree, or the law degree. For example, in one case, a couple who were both medical students agreed that the husband would finish his education first while the wife supported him. When he finished, she would complete her education.

After his first year of residency, the couple separated. The court held that the husband's medical school degree and license to practice medicine were obtained during the marriage, and therefore were "property" and to be considered assets to be divided. It established the value of the husband's medical education as the difference in earning capacity between a man with a four-year college degree and a specialist in internal medicine. With the help of a financial analyst, the court valued the education at $306,000. The wife was awarded, in addition to alimony, 20 percent of this amount over a five-year period.

▶ On the Road with a Family Business: How to Divide *This* Asset?

Whenever one of the marital assets in a divorce is a business, there are challenges in dividing this asset. A business can be a dental, medical, law, or accounting practice; a real estate firm; or a home-based business. It can be a sole proprietorship, a partnership, or a corporation.

Stop #1: Value the Business

If you or your spouse have a small business, a family business, or a closely held business, you need to know what that business is worth, and you may need to bring in a business appraiser to help with this evaluation. If you know that the business creates cash flow, it's definitely worth looking into. If you know that it's barely making it, or running into financial loss, strongly consider where you want to spend your investigative monies.

A business appraiser will look at the revenues, expenses, type of industry, equipment and other asset values, even the economic impact on the local, state, or national economies. Many items outside of the net worth or book value of the business are also considered. *Never* use any value that is provided by the business's accountant or CPA. There are many ways to value a business.

Business appraisers sometimes have to do their own sleuthing. For small businesses, especially cash businesses (e.g., restaurants, cafés, bars, salons, a store where one of the spouses is a partner), individuals or investigators are hired to actually sit in the business, use its services, and buy its products. Why? To help determine how much cash is flowing through. The accountant can then verify if those purchases appear on reported gross receipts. If they don't, you have confirmation that skimming or nonreporting of income is

In a divorce, most businesses should be appraised.

occurring. The next step is to determine what percentage or amount is involved.

You want someone who specializes in evaluating businesses or, better yet, in evaluating your type of business. Most likely, your appraiser will be a member of one of various appraisers' organizations (see Appendix B for a list). The cost for an appraisal of a small business can range from $5,000 or up; for a larger business, it's not unusual to see tens of thousands of dollars charged.

Don't Be Penny Wise and Pound Foolish: A Rubbernecking Case Study.

Becky and James decided to divorce after 35 years of marriage. James owned a heavy construction business and he agreed to split the business assets 50-50. The company CPA had placed a value on it of $300,000.

At first, this seemed fair enough but then Becky started thinking. She told her attorney, "I used to keep the books for the business. I can remember taking in more than a million dollars each year. I think the company CPA has purposely lowballed the value. Do you think the business is only worth $300,000?"

Not likely. Becky's attorney insisted that she have the business appraised. The appraisal cost her $4,300, an amount that seemed huge to her and made her nervous. What if the business was only worth $300,000? She would have kissed off the $4,300! The appraisal opened her eyes—it valued the company at $850,000! Her investment of $4,300 netted her $275,000 more than she would have received with the $300,000 valuation!

Therefore, when looking at an offer for settlement of a business, ask yourself the following three key questions:

1. Is there something you don't know about that you are leaving on the table? In many states there have been cases where, if one spouse defrauded the other by not revealing information, they went back to the court to have the settlement adjusted.

2. Are you being given truthful information when you look at what's on the table? Are you getting bad data on values?

3. Are you making up a wish list for things that don't really exist?

When looking at a cash-and-carry-type business, you need to determine a range of values. Some of the ways to determine these values include rule-of-thumb multipliers, capitalization rates, defined ratios within the industry, book value, adjusted book value, net book value, replacement value, depreciated value, stock market value, liquidation value, and fair market value. Who knows? There could even be a toss-of-the-coin value.

Usually, good will should be included, especially if the business has been a going concern for a number of years. What is *good will*? A dictionary defines it as the value of a business in patronage, reputation, and established popularity over and beyond its tangible assets—in other words, the perceived public value in excess of cash and equipment and other material items.

Whatever the acceptable value ranges, it's important that you determine whether you are dealing with smaller amounts of money such as in a range of $5,000 to $40,000 or larger amounts that can run in the hundreds of thousands of dollars. Once you know an estimated value range, you can then determine how much money you are willing to spend to go after the business. Remember, Becky was antsy about spending $4,300 on a business that was worth hundreds of thousands of dollars. On the other hand, it's crazy to spend thousands of dollars when the business may only be worth a few thousand.

A complication rears its head. You need to determine whether the data you receive is valid. This could come partly from your own intuition and practical observation about what kind of lifestyle you have been living. Talk to employees, colleagues, and associates, and use your direct information —things that you had a hands-on relationship with.

Stop #2: Divide the Business

Dividing up a business is another issue. There are four options when deciding how to go about doing it:

1. One spouse keeps the business.
2. One buys the other out.
3. Both spouses keep the business.
4. Both spouses sell the business outright and split the proceeds.

If one spouse is the primary driver in keeping and running the business, you will probably know early on in your divorce process which spouse will continue with the business by buying it or giving assets of equal value. If there are no assets large enough to give, a property settlement note could be created or a loan obtained. If the other spouse owns shares of the company, the company could buy back those shares over time.

However, be careful when buying out or selling shares of stock. If there has been an increase in the value of the stock, the selling spouse could be liable for capital gains tax. On the other hand, if one spouse buys the shares directly from the other, it would be considered a transfer of property incident to divorce, which is not a taxable issue.

If you and your spouse have worked next to each other every day for many years, it is obviously much more difficult to divide a family-owned business. Both of you may have emotional ties to the business. In addition, if you try to divide your business, it may kill the business. On the other hand, some couples are better business partners than marriage partners, and they are able to continue to work together in a business after the divorce is final. This doesn't work for everyone, but should be considered as an option.

Some couples opt to sell the business and divide the profits; this way, both are free to look elsewhere for other employment, another business, or even to retire. The problem here may be in finding a buyer. Sometimes it takes years to sell a business. In the meantime, you and your spouse need to make decisions as to whose business it is and who runs it.

Stop #3: Embark on a Scavenger Hunt

Discovering and determining what property should be identified as marital assets takes a little work. At times, it may seem as though you've been sent on a scavenger hunt to find assets. The following paragraphs are a quick review of places to look when investigating the value of a business.

Tax returns. They show interest and dividend income and name the source. Look at Schedule B. If you see $5,000 interest from a mutual fund or bond, you know someplace there is an asset worth about $62,500 (if it is yielding 8 percent). If instead that $5,000 is from a bank or credit union, it is probably earning more like 4 percent and the asset may be worth about $125,000.

Financial statements. When used to secure a loan, these usually have values assigned to assets to pump up the net worth. If your spouse was trying to impress the bank with your combined net worth, there may be some assets there worth tracking down.

Canceled checks. A large sum made out to a brokerage firm, mutual fund, or insurance company would indicate that an investment was made. And that money is sitting someplace even though you may not have known about it. Make sure when looking through the checks that you have all of them and there are no missing numbers.

Copies of investment statements. This will show values. If you have several months of statements and you see that the value declined within the past few months due to a withdrawal, find out where that money went. It may be sitting in a different account someplace else. You may even need to look back years.

Deferred compensation. Did your spouse talk about an expected bonus that somehow never got paid? Perhaps the bonus is still owed but the company is helping out by holding that bonus until after the divorce is over. Check it out!

Cash business. Does your spouse own a business that takes in a lot of cash? It is important to know how much cash flow there really is.

Retirement plans. These are biggies. Remember that in most states, retirements plans are marital property even if held in only one name. It is important to have the paperwork on each one.

Payroll stubs. Is your spouse having money withheld that goes into a special account nobody else knows about?

Contracts or agreements that pay out in the future on work done in the past. Because the work was done during the marriage, the future payout is marital property. This category includes royalties, patents, and commissions.

▶ Check Your Rearview Mirror: Review All Financial Records

During your divorce, you may harbor suspicions, right or wrong, that your spouse is hiding assets. And you may very well be right. Assets are traditionally hidden in one of four ways:

1. By denying the existence of an asset
2. By transferring it to a third party
3. By "claim offset" (which means the asset exists but was diverted)
4. By claiming the asset was lost or dissipated

In addition to these, there is a new way to hide assets: by creating false debt. This means that loans and other obligations may suddenly appear. For example, suppose your spouse claims that $10,000 is owed to Dad. You had thought it was a gift to the two of you; now that you're getting divorced, it's a loan—which means it's not part of the assets to be divided.

Search the Back Roads

The sooner you learn about your and your spouse's assets, the better. Once one of you moves out, so do many of the marriage assets, especially when it comes to personal items. By now, you may have learned of assets you previously didn't know were assets. Most marriages have hidden loot. In many cases, each partner has a different perception of its value. So you need to go on a scavenger hunt to protect your assets so that they can be divided fairly.

Even if your spouse has planned to leave you for quite a while, if you're still living together, copy every financial record you can find. Copy any bank or other financial account numbers and make copies of the statements; it makes tracking and verification easier. Keep in mind that you're on shaky ground if you open mail that is identified as separate property, even if you steam it or rip it open and claim it was an accident. So don't do anything illegal: instead, write down the date that you received it and copy the envelope.

The IRS has a special form that will allow you to obtain past tax returns. This might take a couple of months, so the sooner you get going, the better. Note bank statements and bank account numbers. Accounts have probably been moved, but if you had a joint account, you've got the number. Ask for copies from the bank for the last five years. Expect a charge—after all, they are not going to do anything for free.

Ask your attorney about changing the door locks and the garage door opener code. You don't want to risk anything leaving your home if your spouse is moving out. It is amazing how objects, artwork, and the like suddenly disappear after a couple files for divorce. Find out if any large sums have been withdrawn from your bank accounts. Ditto for any stock or other investment-related accounts.

Reconstruct Your Financial Life. As you obtain bank statements, bills, and any correspondence that refers to assets and income, you should begin the next critical step—sitting down and starting to reconstruct your financial life. First, evaluate your expenses, and try not to guess. Ideally, it makes sense to know where monies were spent for an entire year. If you don't have access to all your records, three months usually gives a good snapshot. Get copies of checking account(s) statements from the bank and credit card statements on cards used during the year, and you will likely be able to determine how much money was spent.

Determine whether you normally spend $1,000 a month or $7,000 a month. How much cash do you personally use? How much walking-around money does your spouse have? In the past, did cash tend to come home in the evening? If you or your spouse owns a business, and there is always cash around, it is *important* to note this. Carry around a small note pad and start taking notes. It is amazing what can jump into your mind at the oddest moments and, if you don't write it down, you're likely to forget it.

Gather up canceled checks, charge receipts, and cash receipts if you have them. Allocate them to specific areas: housing, utilities, automotive, insurance (auto, medical, dental, life, disability, homeowners, fire, etc.), retirement funds, entertainment, education, contributions, charge accounts, wardrobe, cleaning, pets, dues, subscriptions, education (yours and the kids'), food, dining out, medical, dental, prescriptions, vacations, gifts, travel related to business, taxis, tips, and rentals. Don't forget ATM receipts—what did you do with the money after you withdrew it?

This probably seems overwhelming, but it has to be done. If you don't have computer access, get a multicolumn spreadsheet, or simply divide a sheet of paper into columns headed "auto, housing," etc. Also, break out expenses for the kids in a separate column/category. For charged items, make sure you put the entire amount charged, not the minimum amount to pay per month on a greater balance. Remember, you are identifying exactly how much you spend each month.

Did you enter your marriage with any separate property, or did you receive any gifts during your marriage—e.g., money, jewelry, houses, apartments, stocks, bonds, artwork, bicycles, furniture, etc.? Any item that you owned prior to your marriage or were given during your marriage may still be separate property. In other words, it is yours and is not included when joint assets are divvied up.

Stay Focused on the Task. Do everything you can to put aside your emotions. Right now, you are simply gathering facts. If your spouse has business partners or colleagues, go see them right away. More than likely, they're not going to be terribly positive about you and probably won't want to talk to you; so don't expect much warmth. Still, your intent is to put them on notice that you certainly don't want to cause any harm, but you want the truth to come out about your financial affairs. You are glad to allow the divorce (assuming they know about it), but you want to make sure that whatever the two of you own is going to get split equally.

In other words, the business partners and colleagues are now on notice that there could be an investigation into assets and income. If they are thinking of any hanky-panky in terms of helping your spouse hide some assets, they'll now know that it is totally unacceptable. By doing this, you let them know you're not a dummy and that you are aware that the business may be involved in the divorce.

The issue here is not for you to know the law. Instead, you are stanching the flow of money very quickly. You want to retain information—and assets. It is not legal for your spouse to strip all your assets; still, you need to know that this could happen.

Also, this is not the time to go about refinancing your home unless you can control the extra funds that come out of it. Nor should you enter into any investments that might demand future payments, or even cosign a loan. Your objective is to become *less liable* for things as you move through this stage of your divorce.

Check Your Insurance Policies. The obvious ones include whole life insurance policies, especially old policies with face values of $1,000, $5,000, and $10,000. They often contain many thousands of dollars in cash value that have been earning a very low interest rate.

If you know of any policies that are in your spouse's name (or yours, for that matter), write the representative or the insurance company, indicate the policy number, and state that you are completing updated financial statements and need to include their value for the bank's purposes. You should expect a reply within a few weeks. This doesn't mean that you are going to cash the policies out—it's merely for your own information.

Today's computers can cross-search names as well as addresses. Don't forget to check for liens or loans against your own house.

Check your homeowner's insurance policy to see if there are addenda to cover extra items, including your jewelry, artwork, and furs if you have any. For example, one woman whose husband collected trains was elated when she discovered a $30,000 addendum to cover their value. That was the key that led to her valuation. Not wanting to part with his toys, he gave her the house as a trade-off.

What to Pack

Documents Describing Your Property that You Should Review with Your Attorney

Do yourself (and your attorney) an enormous favor by assembling the following before your initial appointment:

▶ *Your check registers or bank statements for the past few years.* If you have your financial information or your check register on a computer program like Quicken, print a copy, make a copy onto a disk, and hold it for safekeeping.

▶ *Any prenuptial or postnuptial agreements.* Gather up any agreements that were drawn up prior to your marriage, or even during your marriage that might designate how assets were to be split or identified, or which designate proportions on earnings for either one of you. If you and your spouse signed a prenuptial agreement, this is a critical document. Its terms will affect many of the issues you must face. In fact, it may mean that there is little, if anything, left to resolve.

▶ *A complete household inventory.* Take pictures. If you have a video camera (you can rent one), don't forget to open up closet doors and take sweeping shots of your living room, dining room, wall hangings, floor coverings, even your outdoor patio. When in doubt, aim the camera and push the button.

▶ *Tax returns that show depreciation schedules as well as gross revenues.* Ask your (or your spouse's) accountant or bookkeeper for copies of their work papers. As mentioned, the IRS has a form you can sign to acquire past tax returns if you don't have them. Make sure that you have at least five years' returns.

▶ *Partnership tax returns.* If you have invested in any partnerships, contact the general partner and get a full copy of the partnership tax return. Ask the person who sold you the investment for an updated evaluation.

▶ *Annual bank, savings, and investment statements.* Most recap additions and withdrawals at the end of the year. Don't forget business-type credit cards. Diners Club and American Express send out year-end statements summarizing charges into various categories.

▶ *A copy of the corporate tax return for any family businesses/corporations.* If the business is filed on a Schedule C within your own tax return, make sure you know, or better yet, obtain copies of the work papers that consisted of the expenses and revenues that constituted the entire schedule. Your accountant can be helpful here. If you feel some resistance in getting the information you request, just say you are getting ready to spread expenses for next year and you would like to have some guidelines on what was done the previous year.

▶ *Financial statements to banks.* These reveal a lot of information, often most optimistic. Few business owners hide how well their businesses are doing; rather, they brag about what they own. If you need to, call the bank and tell them you're doing updated financial statements and you have lost copies of previous ones. Ask them to send you a copy so that you could make sure that you do not exclude anything.

▶ *Warranty deeds, contracts, title insurance, and other real estate documents.* This should include any documents that establish ownership to investments and real estate other than your residence, including any preliminary title searches showing other ownership and any deeds (first, second, even third trust deeds) or sales contracts on real estate.

▶ *Title certificates and registration statements for vehicles.* This includes boats, cars, recreational vehicles, trucks, etc. Also include an estimate of the value of your automobiles. In evaluating cars, call the local bank and say that you are interested in purchasing whatever the car is that you and your spouse currently own. Ask for the high and low *Kelley Blue Book* values. Ask if they would be receptive to financing the car. If that feels uncomfortable, call the bank and say that you are completing a net-worth statement and you don't know what value to put on your car. Could they look it up in their *Blue Book?* Or, visit the library or go online to find the *Kelley Blue Book* (www.autoweb.com). If your car is older and not carried, check the classified ads in your newspaper. You may own a classic! Edmunds.com is a great source for auto valuations.

▶ *List of all current debts, monthly payments, and reason for the debt.* This includes any notes payable to you or payable by you.

▶ *Any retirement, pension, or profit-sharing plans.* This includes IRAs; Keoghs; and brokerage, bank and money market fund statements. Financial institutions and employers who have pension and profit-sharing programs send out at least annual statements. Get copies when possible.

▶ *Insurance policies.* Make copies of all personal and business insurance policies.

▶ Traveling to the Poor House: Handling Debt, Credit Problems, and Bankruptcy

Just as property is either marital or separate, the same classifications apply to debt. In general, both you and your spouse are responsible for any debts incurred during your marriage—regardless of who really spent the money. When your property is divided up during the divorce, the person who gets the asset usually also gets the responsibility for any loans against it.

What to Pack

Financial Documents and Information You Need to Gather

▶ *For owners of a small business, copies of all journals and general ledgers.*
Don't overlook any accounts receivable, works in progress, inventory, or
bank statements. Payroll and sales tax returns give a lot of information.
Some attorneys will recommend that you get a copy of the corporate
minutes book and the stock books. Our experience has been that many
small businesses ignore these and fill these in after the fact, often several
years down the road, if they are needed for an audit. Not that they are
supposed to do it this way; it's just one of those "I'll get to it" projects.

▶ *A copy of your spouse's previous month's payroll stub (preferably at least
three months' worth).* Why? Because not all items are deducted from each
paycheck. Sometimes it is every other paycheck, other times, it's once a
month. Call the payroll department where your spouse works and ask them
to explain it to you.

    For example, one woman called her husband's accountant and merely
said she was getting more involved in the finances and that she needed
to have her husband's payroll stub explained to her. By the time she was
done, in addition to the normal deductions for federal and state taxes and
Social Security, she discovered that her husband was setting aside $500
a month in a tax-sheltered annuity, was paying one of the car loans, and
had an extra savings account, as well as excess contributions based on a
percentage formula in retirement programs. If she hadn't done that, she
very well could have missed out on thousands of dollars in hidden assets.

▶ *All W-2 statements that were filed with the last tax return.* Note if there is
any difference in the amount from which federal taxes are withheld and
the amount on which Social Security is based. If the Social Security wage
base number is higher than the reportable W-2 earnings for tax purposes,
you know that funds are being placed in either a tax-sheltered annuity or a
401(k) program where federal and state taxes are deferred until they are
withdrawn. Social Security tax, though, is not deferred, and is calculated
on earnings on an ongoing basis. Both annuities and 401(k) plans offer the
ability to defer taxes on current income.

▶ *Copies of any records relating to savings and credit union accounts, bank
statements, and any royalty payments.* If your spouse is an author or
artist, you may be entitled to a portion of what is completed, regardless of
whether the work has been sold.

▶ *Any certificates that show values of gems, antiques, artwork.* This should
include anything collectible (refer back to Roadmap 2.1 to double check
these).

▶ *Monies that are placed in tax-exempt investments.* These are often difficult to track. It is imperative for you to get at least the past five years of statements and tax returns if this is one of the possible areas in which investments are placed.

▶ *Interest earned from Treasury bills and municipal bonds.* If you or your spouse have invested in Treasury bills, the interest received is nontaxable on your state return but is fully taxable on your federal return. If you live in one state and own a municipal bond that was originated in another, the interest is tax exempt on your federal return but taxable on your state return—the opposite of a Treasury bill or bond. This is why you want both federal and state tax returns—to cross-check income that is reported.

▶ *Documentation of any investment.* Anything in which monies have been placed for creating income investment growth needs to be checked and tracked down.

▶ *Patent applications, license rights, or royalty agreements.* These are important if your spouse is an inventor.

▶ *An estimate of your spouse's salary (if you don't know).* If you are unclear as to what your spouse makes (this assumes you don't have W-2s or payroll stubs), get a copy of tax returns from the IRS. If, for some reason, that's not possible, check publications such as *Fortune* or *Forbes* or trade publications for your spouse's profession. They publish annual surveys of what various positions and industries pay. Or search the Internet (even if you don't have a computer, most libraries have computers available to the public), go to "key word" and then type in various words that fit your spouse's job title and query for salary range. If you know anyone who works in the executive-search field or in a job placement agency, they could estimate your spouse's earning power. If you don't, call one and say that you are doing some research on career opportunities and ask if they could give you some guidelines on what to expect.

▶ *A copy of any employment contracts.* They should state clearly not only initial salary, but bonus formulas and stock options.

▶ *Any data that can show that personal expenses or quasi-personal expenses are run through a family business as expenses.* This could be a potential jackpot. Most self-employed taxpayers who are not incorporated report income on Schedule C within their regular tax return. Usually, they report as much as they possibly can as business expenses.

Many of these expenses may be personal. Examples would include travel and entertainment—a huge area that absorbs a lot of personal pleasures both of you may have enjoyed in the past year. Professional services could have included having your will drawn up; the new painting that hangs in your living room could have been expensed under office furniture; the car that you drive may very well be identified as the company car. The list goes on and on.

We know the list of information you should gather in "What to Pack" seems overwhelming, but take a deep breath—a lot of this is merely detail and paperwork. If you would rather pay an attorney big bucks to do it for you, you can. We recommend you don't. Today, judges are reluctant to award any legal fees. You are on your own.

It's usually in the best interests of both of you to pay off as many debts as possible before or at the time of the final decree. To do so, consider whatever liquid assets you have: bank accounts, money market funds, stocks, bonds, or cash values from life insurance to use to pay these debts. It may make sense to sell assets to accumulate some extra cash. The most easily sold assets include extra cars, vacation homes, and excess furniture. (Don't expect to get much for used furniture unless it has value as an antique or collector's piece.)

If you can't pay off your debts, then the decree must state who will pay which debt and within what period of time. There are generally four types of debt to consider: secured debt, unsecured debt, tax debt, and divorce expense debt. Consider these detours on your road to a clean divorce. Each is discussed in the following sections; additional information on protecting your credit is provided in Chapter 5.

Detour #1: Secured Debt

Secured debt includes the mortgage on your home or other real estate, and loans on your cars, trucks, and other vehicles. You and your spouse should make it very clear in your separation agreement *who will pay which debt.* You'll want to refinance these debts into your respective names or pay them off as soon as possible, because if one of you fails to make a payment on a jointly held debt that is secured by an asset, the creditor will come after the asset securing the debt or the creditor can pursue the other ex-spouse.

Detour #2: Unsecured Debt

Unsecured debt includes credit cards, personal bank loans, lines of credit, and loans from parents and friends. These debts may be divided equitably; the court also considers who is better able to pay the debt.

For unsecured debt, any separation agreement needs to include a *hold-harmless* clause. This will *indemnify* the nonpaying spouse, which means that the paying spouse gives the nonpaying spouse the right to collect not only all missed payments, but also damages, interest, and attorney's fees if pay-

Bactracking

13 Ways to Be a Super Sleuther

1. Make copies of all financial statements.
2. Obtain copies of tax returns.
3. Make duplicate copies of any computer files that relate to ownership and financial matters.
4. Obtain copies of current insurance policies.
5. Obtain copies of any wills and trusts.
6. Make an inventory of contents in safety deposit boxes. Take someone with you to witness. Take photos.
7. Contact the county assessor to get a copy of any deeds and titles for real estate owned.
8. If you own a small business, get copies of financial journals, ledgers, payroll, sales tax returns, and expense account disbursements.
9. Obtain copies of any appraisals for artwork, antiques, jewelry, and other collectibles.
10. Videotape your entire house, including contents of closets.
11. Obtain information on pensions for both you and your spouse.
12. Obtain copies of at least three of your spouse's recent pay stubs.
13. Obtain a current report of earnings from your local Social Security office for both of you.

ments are not made. Without a hold-harmless clause, the nonpaying spouse has the right to collect only the missed payments.

Often, the legal decision and the financial outcome are very different things. For example, consider this scenario. Tracy and Paul were married eight years, during which time Tracy ran her credit cards to the limit with her compulsive spending. The court held Tracy solely responsible for paying the $12,000 in credit card debt. After the divorce, however, Tracy didn't change her ways and was unable to pay off her debt. The credit card companies came after Paul, who ended up paying them off.

> *Even though something was agreed on,*
> *it doesn't necessarily happen as planned.*

In a case like this, one solution would have been to pay off the credit cards with assets at the time of the divorce or for Paul to have received more property to offset this possibility. Another solution would have been for Tracy to get Paul's name removed from the debt by refinancing.

Detour #3: Tax Debt

Just because the divorce settlement is final doesn't mean you are exempt from possible future tax debt. For three years after your divorce, the IRS can perform a random audit of your last joint tax return. In addition, the IRS can question a joint return—if it has good cause to do so—for seven years. It can also audit a return whenever it believes fraud is involved.

To avoid surprises, your divorce agreement should spell out what happens if any additional interest, penalties, or taxes are found, as well as where the money comes from to pay for defending an audit. There have been countless horror stories where an unsuspecting spouse is suddenly obligated for a huge tax bill and doesn't have a clue how it happened.

Detour #4: Divorce Expense Debt

Although it isn't always clear who is liable for debts incurred during the separation, typically these debts are the responsibility of the person who incurred them. An exception would be if one of you runs up debts that you are unable to pay to buy food, clothing, shelter, or medical care for your kids. The other spouse is probably obliged to pay those expenses.

> *If you paid some divorce expenses before the divorce process officially started, you will want to get a credit offset for these expenses in the final agreement.*

You will accrue other costs during the divorce process, including court filing fees, appraisals, mediation, and attorneys. Other less obvious expenses are accounting, financial planning, and counseling. The separation agreement needs to state very clearly who is responsible for these expenses.

Divorce expenses may accrue after the decree, such as attorney fees for doing QDROs, title transfers, tax preparation for the final joint tax return, mediation fees, and long-term divorce counseling for you and your ex-spouse or your kids. Who pays? *You do,* unless it is spelled out clearly so there are no disputes at a later date.

Detour #5: Dividing Marital Property and Debts

Many people try to divide each asset as they discuss it—e.g., "your half of the house is $4,000, my half of the house is $4,000." Because you will rarely divide a house like this, this may not be the most useful way to go about it. It may be more practical to list each asset as a whole item under the name of the person who will keep it.

For example, in the wife's column, list the marital equity in the house if she is thinking of continuing to live there. List the entire value of the husband's retirement in his column, if that is your initial inclination. An advantage to this method is that it allows you to see the balance, or lack of it, of your initial plan as you develop it (as shown earlier in this chapter). If you want to know dollar values, you may need a third party, such as an appraiser, to help you determine them.

This is the time to have a real heart-to-heart discussion with your soon-to-be-ex about the range of fair division. Ask the following questions:

1. Is the only possibility for a 50-50 division of things by value? By number?
2. Are you more interested in cash than in things?
3. Will you take less than 50 percent if your share is all cash?
4. Are you more interested in *future* security than in *present* assets?
5. Are you willing to wait for a buyout of your share, such as selling the house or retirement, and are you looking for more than 50 percent to compensate you for waiting?
6. Are you interested in a "lopsided" agreement (i.e., more to one of us than the other) to compensate for the larger earnings made by you or your spouse?
7. Do you want to be "made whole"—meaning ending up where you were at the beginning of your relationship?
8. Do you need to be compensated "off the top" for some contribution you made to the acquisition of property?
9. Is there a possibility that any assets or investments are hidden?

If you can agree on a generic plan that meets each of your ideas of fairness, you will find you have an agreement that practically writes itself. The bonus is that you'll save on lawyer's fees!

As you allocate your debts, decide first whether they are marital, separate, or a mix. Then agree who will pay off the balance of each. Remember

Bactracking

13 Points to Keep in Mind When Dividing Property

1. All earned income acquired during your marriage, no matter whose name it's in, is considered to be marital property, unless there is a prenuptial agreement stating otherwise.
2. A property settlement note can be used to even up a property division and should be collateralized.
3. Be careful when dividing assets if one spouse gets all the cash while the other spouse gets assets that are not liquid (such as real estate) or all retirement funds, which, when taxes are deducted, are not worth as much.
4. The expert who appraises your family business should not work for that business.
5. If your house has a large capital gain, take that into account when dividing the rest of your assets.
6. Even if your desire to keep your house is emotional, get some advice on the financial ramifications of keeping it.
7. If your spouse declares bankruptcy, any alimony and child support awarded will not be affected.
8. Most household furniture is valued at garage-sale value.
9. Any cash-value life insurance purchased with marital assets is considered· property to be divided.
10. A gift or inheritance received during your marriage and kept in your name only should be considered your separate property.
11. If you or your spouse supported the other through college education or built a career, that may have value as property.
12. Before alimony is awarded, all property is divided.
13. The 1997 tax law created a $250,000 per-person ($500,000 per couple) exclusion when selling the home. It can be reused every two years.

that the problem of unsecured debts may be handled more easily as if it were a monthly credit card payment than a division of your property.

Think about the long-term effect of the division of assets and debts you are considering. For example, suppose you get all assets that appreciate slowly or depreciate, and that also take money to maintain (e.g., home, car, furniture). Suppose your spouse takes all assets that increase in value or produce income (stock, retirement accounts, rental home). Guaranteed, in a few years after the divorce, what in the short term appeared to be "fair" or "equal" will look quite different. Your spouse's net worth will far exceed yours—and the gap will just continue to widen.

Detour #6: Dealing with Bankruptcy

The word *bankruptcy* strikes fear in the hearts of many people—especially those going through divorce. You may be trying to decide whether it is better to ask for alimony or a property settlement note and are caught in indecision. Perhaps your spouse has threatened either to leave the country if alimony is required or to file bankruptcy if money is owed or a property settlement note is due. Let's look at some of the rules of bankruptcy as they apply in divorce situations.

There are two types of bankruptcy available:

1. Chapter 13 bankruptcy allows you to *develop a payoff plan* over a three-year period. It may preserve your assets and allow the debtor (i.e., you or your spouse) to pay off all the secured debt, as well as a portion of the unsecured debt, and discharge the rest of the unsecured debt. The debtor needs to make payments under a plan that is approved by the bankruptcy court.

2. Chapter 7 bankruptcy allows you to *liquidate all of your assets* and use the proceeds to pay off debts, erasing debts that cannot be paid in full. It forgives all unsecured debts and requires the forfeiture of all your assets over certain minimum protected amounts. Creditors have the right to repossess their fair share of the assets. The net proceeds from the sale of assets are divided *pro rata* among the creditors.

Here are some things to remember:

▶ If one of you files bankruptcy before, during, or after divorce, the creditors of jointly held debts will seek out the other spouse for payment—no matter what was agreed to in the separation agreement.

▶ While you are still married, you can file for bankruptcy jointly. This will eliminate all separate debts of the husband, separate debts of the wife, and all jointly incurred marital debts.

Driving Solo to Retirement

Dividing Pensions and Retirement Plans

Pensions and other retirement plans are recognized as part of the joint property acquired during the marriage and as part of the assets to be divided when a couple divorces. A non-wage-earning spouse typically is entitled to a portion of the pension of a working spouse. The portion of that pension fairly attributable to a non-wage-earning spouse is based on the present value of the future pension, adjusted by the ratio of years worked while married to total years worked. Also, even a wage-earning spouse may be entitled to a portion of his or her ex-spouse's retirement benefits. Pension and retirement benefits earned during the marriage are potentially of great value. In a longer marriage, they may be the most valuable asset that the couple owns, so this chapter describes in detail how to make sure you get what you're entitled to.

Consult an experienced financial professional, such as a Certified Divorce Financial Analyst, to determine this value and the right documentation for the court and employer. To ensure that a person receives a fair share of the ex-spouse's pension, the court can issue a Qualified Domestic Relations Order (QDRO, discussed in detail in this chapter), which legally divides the pension into two pieces, with each piece owned by the respective ex-spouse.

Without the QDRO executed correctly, the ex-spouse will likely lose all rights to the pension. Don't let this happen! Read on.

▶ A Fork in the Road: Two Ways to Divvy Pensions

There are two main schools of thought when it comes to dividing pension benefits:

1. The *buy-out* or *cash-out* method, which awards the nonemployee spouse a lump-sum settlement—or a marital asset of equal value—at the time of divorce, in return for the employee's keeping the pension.
2. The *deferred division* or *future share* method, where no present value is determined—each spouse is awarded a share of the benefits if and when they are paid.

In a defined-contribution retirement savings plan, there is very little problem identifying the value of the account. Monthly or quarterly statements show the dollar amount available to be divided in either the buy-out method or the future share method. To understand this better, you need to know the difference between the two main types of retirement or pension plans: defined-contribution and defined-benefit. The following sections describe some ways to split up the treasure chest.

Route 1: Divvying a Defined-Contribution Retirement Savings Plan

The 401(k) is one type of defined-contribution retirement plan. But even in the overall group of 401(k)s, there are different types with different rules. Each company can set its own rules for its retirement plans—as long as the plan is approved by the IRS.

Let's look at some hypothetical examples that illustrate the defined contribution plans for three employees: Andy, Bob, and Chris. Each participates in a defined-contribution plan, yet has different results.

Scenario #1. Employee A (Andy) Is Married and Works for a Company that Has a 401(k). He puts all his retirement money into the 401(k) and the company does not match any of his funds. He has worked there for three years and has accumulated $1,500 in his plan.

Any money that Andy puts into his 401(k) is his: he is 100 percent vested. If he quits or is fired, he can take all this money with him. He can use it as

Tollbooth 3.1

Marital Portion of a 401(k) Retirement Plan

	Andy
Length of Employment	3 years
401(k) Value at Time of Divorce	$1,500
Percent Vested	100%
Marital Portion	$1,500

income, declaring such to the IRS (and most likely, receiving a penalty of 10 percent of the withdrawn amount and paying federal and state income taxes on the entire amount at the time of withdrawal) or he can roll it over to an IRA.

After a three-year marriage, Andy and his wife begin the divorce process. Tollbooth 3.1 shows what Andy's retirement savings plan looks like.

Scenario #2: Employee B (Bob) Works for a Company Where only the Employer Contributes Money to the 401(k). Bob doesn't put anything in. Like Andy, Bob has worked there for three years and his 401(k) is worth $1,500. The company uses a vesting schedule, which regulates how much money he can take with him if he quits or is fired.

The amount depends on how long he has worked for the company. Bob is 30 percent vested. Therefore, his 401(k) today is worth 30 percent of $1,500, or $450. The lower amount, $450, is assigned to the marital pot of assets. Tollbooth 3.2 shows how Andy's and Bob's retirement plans compare.

Tollbooth 3.2

How Vesting Affects the Marital Portion of Retirement Plans

	Andy	Bob
Length of Employment	3 years	3 years
Value at Time of Divorce	$1,500	$1,500
Percent Vested	100%	30%
Marital Portion	$1,500	$450

Tollbooth 3.3

How Different Vesting Levels and Matching Contributions Affect the Marital Portions of Different Retirement Plans

	Andy	Bob	Chris
Employee/Employer Contribution	n/a: 0	$1,500	$1 + 50 cents match
Length of Employment	3 years	3 years	3 years
Value at Time of Divorce	$1,500	$1,500	$1,500
Percent Vested	100%	30%	30%
Marital Portion	$1,500	$450	$1,000 + $150 =1,150

Scenario #3: Employee C (Chris) Works for a Company that Matches Every Dollar He Puts into the 401(k) with 50 Cents. Like Andy and Bob, Chris has also worked at his company for three years and he has $1,500 in his 401(k). Out of $1,500, he has put in $1,000 and the company has put in $500 with its matching program. Chris is 30 percent vested. However, the $1,000 that he put in was his money, so he is 100 percent vested in that amount and he can take that whole $1,000. He can take 30 percent of the $500—or $150. Chris's marital portion of this 401(k) is worth $1,150. Tollbooth 3.3 shows how the combination of different vesting levels and matching contributions affect the marital portion of a retirement plan.

Keep these three scenarios in mind when you and your soon-to-be-ex-spouse are reviewing your retirement plans, so you'll know what to expect in terms of the marital portion to be paid.

Route 2: Divvying a Defined-Benefit Retirement Savings Plan

A defined-benefit retirement plan promises to pay the employee a certain amount per month at retirement time. In many pensions, there are choices as to how it will be paid out, known as *life, years certain, life of employee and spouse,* etc. Based on a predetermined plan formula—not from an account balance—comes the company's guarantee to pay the value of a defined-benefit plan.

For instance, the amount of the monthly pension payment could be determined by a complex calculation that includes any or all of the following factors:

▶ the employee's final average salary,
▶ an annuity factor based on the employee's age at retirement,
▶ the employee's annual average Social Security tax base,
▶ the employee's total number of years of employment and age at retirement,
▶ the method chosen by the employee to receive payment of voluntary and required contributions, and
▶ whether a pension will be paid to a survivor upon the employee's death.

As you might guess, the valuation of such a plan poses a challenge and has fostered much creativity!

How Qualified Domestic Relations Orders (QDROs) Affect the Payout in a Defined-Benefit Plan. To see how a defined-benefit plan works, let's look at the example of Henry and Ginny. Assume that, based on today's earnings and his length of time with the company, Henry will receive $1,200 a month at age 65 from his pension. He is now age 56, and he has to wait nine more years before he can start receiving the $1,200 per month. Because of the wait, it is called a future benefit. The value of a future benefit is determined by mathematical assumptions and calculations.

It is important to find out whether the $1,200 per month that he will get at age 65 is based on today's earnings and time with the company, or whether the $1,200 per month includes built-in projected earnings if he stays with the company until age 65. If it is not clear on the pension statements, you must ask these questions of the plan administrator.

If the couple has fewer than eight years to wait until retirement, Ginny may choose to wait to get the $600 per month so she can have guaranteed income. However, if they are nine or more years away from retirement, she may wish to trade out another asset up front. This way, she'll be assured of getting some funding.

Assume that Ginny decides to wait nine years until Henry retires to receive her benefit. They have been married 32 years. Instead of stating in the QDRO that she will receive $600 per month, it may be more prudent to use a formula that states she will receive a percentage or half of the following:

$$\frac{\text{Number of years married while working}}{\text{Total number of years worked until retirement}} = \frac{32}{41}$$

If Henry's final benefit would pay him $1,800 per month:

$$32 \div 41 \times \$1,800 \div 2 = \$702$$

This may be a more equitable division of the pension based on the premise that Ginny was married to Henry during the early building-up years of the plan.

It is also important to ascertain if the plan will pay Ginny at retirement time (when Henry is 65) even if Henry doesn't retire. He may decide *not* to retire just so Ginny can't get her portion of his retirement plan! Some companies do allow the ex-spouse to start receiving benefits at retirement time even if the employee has not retired. This depends on the QDRO's dividing method and the plan—which is one reason to have a pension expert involved in your case.

Hazard!

Pension Pitfalls

The rules that apply to dividing a corporate pension do not apply to government pensions.

A QDRO should only be prepared by an expert who specializes in pensions.

To QDRO or Not to QDRO. The Qualified Domestic Relations Order directs the administrator of a pension plan as to the amount to be paid to the nonemployee spouse after the divorce is final. However, you need to know that many plans don't allow for this order. The parameters and language of a pension plan take precedence over court rulings.

If you or your spouse are participants in any type of pension plan, you need to obtain the plan documents and have them reviewed by an expert to ascertain how that company handles any division of retirement assets. And you should do this *before* your divorce is final.

Bumps in the Road: Common Pension-Related Mistakes

Unfortunately, many lawyers make mistakes in determining the distribution and division of assets, especially in the area of pensions. To help you avoid the pension trap, the following paragraphs list the most common mistakes lawyers make in this area. Certified divorce financial analysts can be extremely helpful in property division analysis. They will augment the work of your attorney.

Mistake #1: Not Identifying All Retirement Plans (Missing a Turnoff). In the discovery process, some lawyers fail to identify all the retirement plans of the other party. This may be due to ignorance, sloppiness, or both.

Mistake #2: Not Understanding the Characteristics of the Retirement Plans (Reading the Map Wrong). Usually through ignorance, lawyers are confused about the different types of retirement plans, and therefore mishandle the division of the retirement. On top of that, few judges are well versed in pensions. They depend on the lawyers in the case to keep the issues straight. You end up with the blind leading the blind.

Hazard!
Protect Your Pension Rights

Do not rely on the judge to keep the pension issues straight. Most of them are just as ignorant as the lawyers and sign whatever order is prepared for them.

▶ If no pension division order is in place after a divorce, the nonemployee has no more rights to the pension than would a total stranger.
▶ Make a priority of getting the pension division order signed at the time of the divorce.

Mistake #3: Waiting Until after the Divorce to Obtain an Approved Order (Running Out of Gas). If the employee dies after the divorce, and no order is in place, the nonemployee spouse will lose every bit of the interest in the employee's retirement. And, if the employee had remarried, the new spouse will receive all the survivor benefits.

If your case involves a pension, discuss this early on and demand that your lawyer give priority to the preparation of a pension division order. If the lawyer does not know how to prepare one, have the lawyer contact a pension order consultant *immediately*. You are forewarned; don't get caught in this abyss!

Mistake #4: Not Taking Responsibility for the Preparation of the Order (Falling Asleep in the Passenger Seat). Even if your lawyer does not know how to prepare the order, you must be the one to find the person to prepare the order, especially if the agreement or decree of dissolution is vague. It makes sense to obtain the advantage for your side when you can.

Mistake #5: Not Anticipating What Will Happen if the Parties Die (Falling Asleep at the Wheel). The order should specify what will happen if death occurs before or during retirement.

Mistake 6: Not Properly Handling Medical Care for the Nonemployee Spouse after the Divorce (Letting the Tires Deflate). This is especially true in governmental plans, where it is frequently possible for the nonemployee to continue coverage indefinitely after the divorce. In each plan, there is a particular process that must be followed, and there are strict deadlines for completing the applications.

▶ A Turn in the Road: Transferring Assets from a Defined Contribution Plan

What happens when an ex-spouse receives the 401(k) asset? There are some specific rules to be aware of. Consider the example of Esther, who was married to an airline pilot nearing retirement. They were both age 55 at the time of the divorce. There was $640,000 in his 401(k) and the retirement plan was prepared to transfer $320,000 to her IRA.

Esther could transfer the money to an IRA and pay no taxes on this amount until she withdrew funds from the IRA. But Esther's attorney's fees were $60,000 and she needed another $20,000 to fix her roof. She said, "I need $80,000." She held back $80,000 of the monies before transferring the remaining $240,000 into her IRA. She was able to spend the $80,000. Esther does have to pay taxes on the $80,000 because she had to declare it as income, but she does not have to pay the 10 percent early-withdrawal penalty.

Normally, distributions made before the participant attains age 59½ are called *early distributions,* and they are subject to a 10 percent penalty tax in addition to any income tax. The penalty tax does not apply to early distributions upon death, disability, annuity payments for the life expectancy of the individual, or distributions made to an ex-spouse by a QDRO.

> *The IRS says that any money received from a qualified plan in a divorce situation may be spent without penalty, even if the recipient is under age 59½.*

After the money from a pension plan goes into an IRA, which is not considered a qualified plan, Esther is held to the early withdrawal rule. If she says, "Oh I forgot, I need another $5,000 to buy a car," it's too late. She will have to pay the 10 percent penalty and the taxes on the monies that were not rolled into the IRA.

It is important to understand the difference between *rolling over* money from a qualified plan and *transferring* money from a qualified plan. The Unemployment Compensation Amendment Act (UCA), which came into effect in January 1993, stated that any monies taken out of a qualified plan or tax-sheltered annuity would be subject to 20 percent withholding. This rule does not apply to IRAs or simplified employee pensions (SEPs).

The following sections describe how this would work.

Exit 1 on the Road to Your Share of a Pension: Transferring Assets via a *Rollover*

Gordon was to receive his ex-wife Yvonne's 401(k) of $100,000, which was invested in the ABC Mutual Fund. He told the 401(k) to send him the money so that he could roll over the proceeds into a different mutual fund of his choice. The 401(k) sent Gordon $80,000, which was the amount remaining after they withheld the 20 percent withholding tax.

Gordon deposited the $80,000 in his new IRA mutual fund. He could have added the $20,000, which was withheld for taxes, but he didn't have $20,000 to spare, even though the IRS would have refunded that amount to him after filing his taxes.

Because he could not come up with the $20,000, the next April when he filed his tax return, he paid an extra $6,600 in state and federal taxes for the

Hazard!

Beware the Tax Collector

To avoid automatic withholding tax, 401(k) transfers must be made directly between trustees and not by a rollover.

"distribution" that was withheld for taxes. Of course, when he eventually takes his IRA money, $20,000 in taxes already will have been paid.

Exit 2 on the Road to Your Share of a Pension: Transferring Assets via a *Direct Transfer*

If Gordon had instead *transferred* the $100,000 from the 401(k) to his new fund, he would have $100,000 in his new fund (instead of $80,000), and he would have *postponed* $6,600 in taxes and saved penalties. It is important to remember the effect of having an extra $20,000 growing tax deferred.

To transfer funds, all Gordon had to do was instruct the 401(k) to send his $100,000 directly to the new IRA account he had just set up with his new mutual fund. Keep this in mind when determining your own transfer of assets from a pension. And, as you've seen in this chapter the mistakes that even divorce lawyers make, recognize that pension distribution is complicated. Get a financial advisor who is expert in this area to help you.

▶ Ease on Down the Road: Update Your Retirement Plans

In addition to determining what you're entitled to from your ex-spouse's retirement plan, you should also update your own retirement plan. Complete the worksheets in Roadmaps 3.2, 3.3, and 3.4 on retirement to project how much money you will need to retire and set up a savings program to meet your goal.

Enroll in all employer-sponsored retirement savings plans, and set aside as much of your salary as you can afford. Set up your own Keogh plan if you earn self-employment income as well as an individual retirement account (IRA). After your divorce, you need to take these steps because you cannot

Roadmap 3.1

12 Important Things to Know about Dividing Pensions

1. In most states, most pensions are treated as marital property to be divided in divorce.

2. To make an intelligent decision on how to divide a pension, it is necessary to understand the *nature* of the pension, how it is *funded*, and how it *pays out*.

3. In most states, a pension can be divided three ways:
   - ▶ value it and trade off assets;
   - ▶ divide it now using a formula approach; or
   - ▶ reserve jurisdiction and divide it when payout to the retiree starts.

4. Different laws and rules apply to dividing *corporate* pensions and *government* pensions.

5. You'd be smart to gather information about the pensions as early in the divorce process as possible.

6. Unless your attorney is very knowledgeable about dividing pensions in divorce, use an expert who specializes in that area.

7. Do not merely follow the pension division order form provided by the plan. It rarely offers all of the choices that you might want to consider in dividing the pension.

8. Have the pension division order in place at the time of your divorce. If a pension division order is not in place when the parties divorce, the nonemployee former spouse has no more rights to the pension than would a total stranger.

9. Plan ahead. Many plan administrators take months to review an order and give feedback on whether it can be implemented.

10. The pension division order should provide for what happens if the employee or nonemployee ex-spouse dies before or after the retirement.

11. Have your attorney take responsibility to prepare the pension division order, even if it means hiring an expert.

12. If you are the nonemployee, make sure you understand the plan's rules about continued coverage under the health care plan.

Roadmap 3.2

Retirement Expenses Worksheet

	Example	Your Situation
1. Present Gross Annual Income	$50,000	$_____
2. Present Annual Savings	$ 5,000	$_____
3. Current Spending (Subtract item 2 from item 1.)	$45,000	$_____
4. Retirement Spending Level (between 80 percent and 100 percent, depending on your lifestyle)	90%	_____%
5. Annual Cost of Living (in Today's Dollars) if You Retire Now (Multiply item 4 by item 3.)	$40,500	$_____
6. 4.5 Percent Inflation Factor (from table below)	2.4	_____
7. Estimated Annual Cost of Living (in Future Dollars) at Retirement (Multiply item 6 by item 5.)	$97,200	$_____

Years until Retirement	Inflation Factor
40	5.8
35	4.7
30	3.7
25	3.0
20	2.4
15	1.9
10	1.6
5	1.2

Roadmap 3.3

Capital Accumulation Worksheet

	Example	Your Situation
1. Estimated Annual Cost of Living (in Future Dollars) at Retirement (item 7 from Retirement Expenses Worksheet)	$ 97,200	$_____
2. Annual Pension Income	10,000	_____
3. Inflation Adjusted Pension Income (Multiply item 2 by appropriate inflation factor in Roadmap 3.2.)	24,000	_____
4. Annual Social Security Benefit	15,000	_____
5. Inflation-Adjusted Social Security Benefit (Multiply item 4 by appropriate inflation factor.)	36,000	_____
6. Inflation-Adjusted Pension and Social Security Income (Add items 3 and 5.)	60,000	_____
7. Amount by Which Expenses Exceed Pension and Social Security Income (Subtract item 6 from item 1.)	37,200	_____
8. Needed Capital (Multiply item 7 by 20.)	$744,000	$_____

Roadmap 3.4

Annual Savings Worksheet

	Example	Your Situation
1. Capital Needed to Fund Retirement (Item 8 from Capital Accumulation Worksheet)	$744,000	$_____
2. Current Investment Assets (Value of Stocks, Bonds, Mutual Funds, and Other Investments)	$30,000	$_____
3. 7.5 percent Appreciation Factor (from table below)	4.2	_____
4. Appreciation of Your Investment Assets until Retirement (Multiply item 2 by item 3.)	$126,000	$_____
5. Other Assets Required by Retirement Age (Subtract item 4 from item 1.)	$618,000	$_____
6. Savings Factor for Years until Retirement (from table below)	.0231	_____
7. Savings Needed over the Next Year (Multiply item 5 by item 6.)	$ 14,276	$_____

Years until Retirement	7.5 percent Appreciation Factor
40	18.0
35	12.6
30	8.8
25	6.1
20	4.2
15	3.0
10	2.1
5	1.4

Years until Retirement	Savings Factor
40	.0044
35	.0065
30	.0097
25	.0147
20	.0231
15	.0383
10	.0707
5	.1722

count on receiving benefits from your ex-spouse's employer-sponsored pension plans or Keogh. Also, you will receive no Social Security benefits based on your former spouse's work record unless you meet several conditions:

1. Your marriage must have lasted at least 10 years.
2. Regardless of the age at which you divorced, to collect you must be at least 62 years old and unmarried.
3. Your ex-spouse must also be at least 62 years old. However, if you have been divorced for at least two years, you can receive benefits even if your ex-spouse is not retired.

Don't feel guilty that the benefits you receive after your divorce will reduce the benefits of your ex-spouse's current mate. The amount of benefits a divorced spouse receives *has no effect* on what a subsequent spouse gets. To find out how much you would receive in divorcee Social Security benefits, call the Social Security Administration (see Appendix B for contact information). If you have also worked, depending on your income and number of work years, you might receive larger benefits if you collected in your own name. Remember to check your options before making a decision. Even if you meet the criteria, don't expect the payments to be generous. You certainly will not be able to live comfortably on these benefits alone.

If you do not qualify for Social Security benefits, your total retirement income must come from your own resources. This includes your savings and investment portfolio, IRA and Keogh plans, defined benefit or defined contribution plans sponsored by your employer, and annuities. Because many people haven't already built up all or even some of these assets and don't attend to it after their divorces, they may live a meager retirement existence.

This is why it is important to set up your own savings plans during your marriage and, if you have not done so, to start investing soon after your divorce. *You* must take charge if you are to enjoy your retirement years! As a retired divorced person, you must make certain lifestyle decisions. Depending on what you can afford later in life, you might move into a continuing-care or another retirement community that offers quality health care and social activities. Because you are no longer married, you cannot rely on your spouse to provide for you, either financially or socially.

Future Tolls

Alimony, Child Support, Taxes

Money is one of the primary factors in and causes of divorce, but it also can be a huge problem *after* divorce. Let's put it this way—it's often the biggest problem. Many people never think about how much money they spend on housing, food, or entertainment. After they divorce, they often find they need to be extremely careful and make an effort to not spend more than they earn. They just don't realize how their finances will change after their divorce, and are therefore forced to cut back substantially and abruptly—on entertaining friends, going out, buying clothes, and other little luxuries. When they first file for divorce, few people expect that this will be how they might have to live.

What's happening here? Why is there no money? Are these people misusing their money? Do they have unreasonable expectations? Or do they just not have enough money? Possibly, the answer is a little bit of everything. We couldn't complete this book without mentioning money—in this case, alimony, also known as spousal support or maintenance. For the payer, it can be a burden. For the receiver, it can be a lifeline—and sometimes a sinker. We'll hit the road with alimony, and move on down and talk about child support and taxes—all essential information you'll need to know to plan your financial life after your divorce.

Dear Ruth,

Since John and I divorced, sometimes I'm so bitter, I can't stand myself. It galls me to know I can't afford the vacations we had in the past, that he can maintain his lifestyle, going everywhere, treating friends to dinners out and entertainment, while I have to count every penny. I'm scared about what will happen to me as I get really old. And the holidays are a disaster: my family isn't together, and I can't afford to buy presents.

I had absolutely no idea of the financial aspects of divorce. I didn't know what to pay anybody. I didn't know it was going to cost so much money. I had no clue how we paid the taxes John reported we paid. I'm always behind on my bills, literally turning into a penny-pincher. I have cut down on everything. I shop for bargains and at discount stores. I used to think having a wallet full of credit cards was my right; now, I have none. I feel like I'm in a marathon race with John for the kids' attention, for their affection, because he can buy them everything. Any suggestions, before I lose my sanity?

—Naomi

▶ Taking the Exit to Alimony: What You Need to Know

For practical purposes, *alimony, maintenance,* and *spousal support* mean the same thing. Simply put, alimony is a series of payments from one spouse to the other, or to a third party on behalf of the receiving spouse. In most cases, the wife is the recipient. You should know that alimony is *taxable income* to the person who receives it and, with few exceptions, for the person who pays it, it's *tax-deductible.*

In a long-term marriage (i.e., more than 10 years) that would be described as "traditional" (meaning the wife has not worked outside the home and has stayed home with kids until they are older or left home), the wife's ability to build a career is somewhat limited. In most cases, if the wife did hold a job, her income was probably less than her husband's, and sometimes substantially lower. If a transfer or move was involved, the decision was probably based on his job and career, so if the couple moved, she usually would have to quit her job and start over somewhere else. This situation is more typical of couples who are over 50 years old. In most marriages of those under 50, both spouses work, and earn comparable salaries; the wife may very well make more than the husband.

Career decisions and divorce can negatively affect the husband, as well. If the wife makes more money, the husband may have refused a job transfer so that his wife could pursue her career. And when they divorce, he can't leave his dead-end job without jeopardizing his pension.

Avoid Road Rage: Know the Criteria for Alimony

Deciding whether a spouse should receive alimony (and if so, how much) is based on certain criteria, and most state statutes give detailed criteria: consult your attorney for details in your state. In the past, fault was the primary factor in determining alimony. Today, in addition to fault, alimony is awarded based on other criteria, including those described in the following paragraphs.

Need (How Much Is Required for One of You to Hit the Road?) To determine need, you need to assess whether or not the recipient of alimony will have enough money to live on after the divorce. If you and your spouse are divorcing amicably, you may be able to make this determination yourselves, by considering each spouse's earning ability, earnings from property received in the property division, and earnings from separate property. If you can't or don't make this determination yourselves, the court will decide for you: alimony may be necessary to prevent the wife (and sometimes the husband) from becoming dependent upon welfare.

Minor children are also considered when evaluating need. Although child support is a separate issue (and discussed later in this chapter), the custodial parent must be able to care adequately for the children. That means keeping a roof over the kids' heads—with utilities to heat, light, and provide water in their home, and food on the table.

However, even though a spouse may think an alimony award is needed, the court sometimes finds otherwise. Take the example of one woman who wanted maintenance from her husband. However, she had a trust of more than $1 million set aside that was separate property. The court believed that she did not need maintenance because she had property that would provide income to her.

Ability to Pay (How Much Money Can a Solo Driver Contribute?) Can the payer afford to pay what is needed and still have enough to live on? The payer's ability to pay may also be based on having enough money left to support a lifestyle roughly equivalent to the marital lifestyle.

Length of Marriage (How Long Have You Been Driving Together?) The longer the marriage, the more likely alimony will be awarded. A two-year marriage may not qualify for alimony, but a 25-year marriage probably would. In addition, the longer the marriage, the longer alimony will be paid.

Previous Lifestyle (How Fancy Was Your Car?) In a 23-year marriage where the husband earns more than $500,000 per year, he probably won't be able to justify a claim that his wife only needs $50,000 per year in alimony. In contrast, if you and your spouse are a young couple who didn't earn much money, you should not expect to become wealthy as a result of your divorce.

Age and Health of Both Parties (What Condition Are You in to Travel?) The following questions are considered when determining whether age or health plays a part in the disposition of alimony:

▶ Are either you or your spouse disabled?

▶ Are either you or your spouse retired? Is there a guaranteed permanent income?

▶ If a wife is 60 years old, does she have a work history? If she has never worked outside the home, it will be very difficult for her to find gainful employment, and permanent alimony is a strong option.

Hazard!

Before You Tie the Knot Again ...

Alimony stops upon the death of the payer. If the recipient remarries, it usually stops.

▶ If you or your spouse is in poor mental or physical health, adequate employment may be difficult to find, and permanent alimony is likely to be granted.

▶ A Fork in the Road: Two Types of Alimony

There are different types of alimony, depending on different circumstances. The following sections describe each.

Route 1: Rehabilitative Alimony

In the 1970s, courts began to recognize the need for a transition period following marriage. It was unrealistic to expect or assume that the wife (or husband, when the wife was the primary or sole breadwinner) could instantly, if ever, earn what her husband did. With that awakening, *rehabilitative* alimony was born.

For example, if you need three years of school to finish your degree or time to update old skills, you may get rehabilitative maintenance. This will give you financial help until you become able to earn enough to support yourself. If you are considering this, stretch your coverage by a few years, if possible. If you have kids, you may take longer to complete a degree or obtain new skills than someone who has no child-care responsibilities.

Route 2: Modifiable versus Non-modifiable Alimony

Given that the one constant thing in life is change, it doesn't make much sense to assume that the final settlement decided in court will apply to all future scenarios. One spouse may become unemployed; the other may become ill. Change can be positive, too: You may land a job that includes lucrative stock options and incentives; you could inherit a substantial sum of money; or win a lawsuit or even the lottery.

To accommodate these potential changes, the court where the divorce is granted often maintains jurisdiction over the case. This allows any order of support to be modified when a change of circumstances makes it reasonable to do so.

These changes in circumstances include increases or decreases in the income or expenses of either or both spouses, especially when such changes are beyond the individual's control.

Hazard!

Non-modifiable Alimony: Friend or Foe?

After the divorce is final and an order of support is given, going the modifiable alimony route, either spouse can go back into court and ask for a modification, either up or down.

What if you get a roommate or cohabit with someone who pays all the expenses? Your ex's attorney could use this fact to reduce current alimony payments. Many states presume that when a spouse who receives alimony moves in with another person, less monetary support is needed.

Be aware that judges do deny requests for modification. Not only that, but they could even rule in the opposite direction! So, before you go back to court to ask for a modification, be sure to examine the position and soundness of your reasons and make sure you have backup evidence to support your requests.

Advantages and Disadvantages of Non-modifiable Alimony. There are certain advantages to non-modifiable alimony. Let's say your divorce decree says you are going to receive six years of alimony that is non-modifiable. This means that even if you get married in two years, you still receive four more years of alimony payments. This also could work against you. What if you become disabled or otherwise need more income? Under the non-modifiable alimony agreement, you can't. When six years are up, all payments stop. Legally, you have no way to continue the alimony income.

What happens if the spouse who is paying alimony retires early and wants to reduce the amount of alimony being paid? To change the original orders, a new court order is needed. That means you go back to court and a judge will make the final decision. You both will have to hire attorneys to represent you. Even if they both agree to modify the original court order, a new agreement must be drawn up.

▶ Paying the Toll: Divorce Is a Taxing Time

To be considered alimony under the tax code, alimony payments must meet *all* of the following requirements:

- ▶ All payments must be made in cash, check, or money order.
- ▶ There must be a written court order or separation agreement.
- ▶ You and your ex can't agree that the payments are *not* to receive alimony tax treatment.
- ▶ You and your ex may not be residing in the same household.
- ▶ The payments must terminate upon the payer's death.
- ▶ You and your *spouse,* if legally separated but not divorced, may not file a joint tax return.
- ▶ No portion of alimony may be considered child support.

Let's look at each requirement in more detail.

Hazard!

Check the Road Conditions Regularly!

Tax laws do change, so check with your tax adviser before filing your return.

Form of Payment: This Toll Is a Cash Lane Only

To qualify as alimony, payments made from one spouse to the other must be made in cash or the equivalent of cash. Transfers of services or property do *not* qualify as alimony.

You can, however, have payments made to a third party on behalf of your spouse and these will qualify as alimony. For example, consider the case of Stanley and Marilyn. Under the terms of their divorce decree, Stanley is required to pay his ex-wife, Marilyn, $5,000 per year for the next five years. Nearly six months after the decree is entered, Marilyn decides to return to school to qualify for a better-paying job. She calls Stanley and asks him to pay her $5,000 tuition instead of sending her the monthly alimony checks. Stanley agrees, and on September 4, 1997, pays $2,500 for Marilyn's first semester tuition. For Stanley to deduct this payment as alimony, he must obtain a *written statement* from Marilyn indicating that they agreed that his payment of the tuition was alimony. (Keep in mind that this tuition payment can be used not only for the spouse receiving alimony, but also for your children's school or college tuition payments.)

This written statement must be received *before* Stanley files his original (not an amended) income tax return for 2005. Here's why. Let's say that as tax return time approaches, Stanley is eager to get his tax refund. On February 14, he files his 2005 return without waiting for the written statement from Marilyn. On March 1, he receives the statement from Marilyn. He may not deduct the payments as alimony because he failed to get the required written statement before the return was filed.

Here's another example of third-party payment. Under the terms of their separation agreement, Robert must pay the mortgage, real estate taxes, and insurance premiums on a home owned solely by his ex-wife, Julia. Robert may deduct these payments as alimony. Julia must include the payments in her income, but she is entitled to claim deductions for the amount of the real estate taxes and mortgage interest if she itemizes her deductions.

One important exception is that payments made to *maintain* property owned by the payer-spouse may not qualify as alimony.

Written Court Order or Separation Agreement: Getting a "License" to Divorce

As mentioned, you must have a written agreement or court order in order for your payments to qualify as alimony (regardless of which spouse is paying). As an example, Craig and Sally are separated. Craig sends Sally a letter offering to pay her $400 a month in alimony for three years. Sally feels this is a slap in the face, because she raised his kids and kept his house clean for 18 years. She does not respond. Craig starts sending the $400 per month. Sally cashes the checks. Because there is no written agreement, Craig may not deduct the payments as alimony.

Here's another example. According to their divorce decree, Allen is to send Marian $750 per month in alimony for 10 years. But two years after their divorce, Marian loses her job and prevails on Allen's good nature to increase her alimony for six months until she gets started in a new job. He starts sending her an extra $200 per month. This was an oral agreement, not a written one. Because no post-decree modification was made, he may not deduct the additional amounts. So make sure you have everything in writing, keep it up to date, and consult your attorney or tax advisor for clarification and assistance.

Taxes: Only One Person Pays the Tolls

Keep in mind that you and your spouse must not opt out of alimony treatment for federal income tax purposes. Maintenance is *taxable* to the person who receives it and *tax-deductible* by the person who pays it.

Cohabitation: Two for the Road

After the final decree, you and your ex-spouse may not be members of the same household at the time payment is made. For example, sometimes a couple gets divorced, but neither can afford to move, so they reach an agreement: she lives upstairs and he lives downstairs. He pays her alimony as specified in the decree, but he cannot deduct it on his tax return. Because this couple still lives in the same house, this payment is not considered alimony. For alimony to be tax deductible, you and your spouse must live in separate homes.

Death of a Spouse: End of the Road for Alimony Payments

The obligation to make payments must terminate upon either spouse's death. Also, when you are planning to divorce, you should consult with an attorney regarding how a divorce will affect your will on *all* financial issues, not just alimony. Depending on your state, a divorce may automatically revoke your entire will or just those parts of it that relate to your former spouse. The bottom line is that you *must* execute new estate planning documents or amend your existing documents if you get divorced.

Joint Tax Returns: The IRS "Exit Ramp" Requires You to File Solo

Many couples file a joint return for the year they got divorced. This is an error. The filing status is the status they have on December 31 of the year they are filing. If you get divorced in 2006, you may not file a joint return for that year, even if you were married for most of that year.

Child Support: When You're on the Road with Kids on Board

If any portion of the maintenance payment is considered to be child support, then that portion cannot be treated as alimony. *Family support* is a common term today. Use it carefully. When alimony is combined with child support, the IRS considers the *entire* payment to be child support. That's great news for the receiver, because the payment does not have to be declared as income. It's bad news for the payer, because *none* of it is deductible from gross income at tax time, whereas alimony alone *is* deductible by the spouse who pays it.

If the separation agreement specifies a certain amount for family support instead of clearly stating a specific amount for *child support* and a specific amount for *alimony,* there could be adverse tax consequences. For example, if the family support is reduced within six months before or after the child reaches the age of majority by the amount that the parents had allocated for child support, the entire amount of the reduction could be deemed child support and nondeductible as alimony. This will be retroactive to the date of the first payment, and any deductions for these payments as alimony will be retroactively disallowed.

Child support is discussed in more detail at the end of this chapter.

▶ Drive Carefully: Protect Yourself by Getting the Necessary Health Insurance

One of the concerns that comes out of a divorce involves health insurance: who pays for it and how does the nonworking spouse continue with coverage? Usually, the greatest impact is for the woman who has had a long-term marriage and is not covered by an employer's health care plan. It is not uncommon for women over 40 to develop severe health problems. Some become almost uninsurable, at least at a reasonable cost. This is a real concern where, all of a sudden, they are on their own and responsible for acquiring health insurance.

The Older Women's League (OWL) worked hard to get the COBRA law passed in 1986. Most people know that COBRA (the Consolidated Omnibus Budget Reconciliation Act) provides that, if an employee is fired or leaves a job, the company can provide health insurance for 18 months. However, in a divorce, the *nonemployee former spouse coverage* is extended to three years (36 months). It allows a nonemployee former spouse (it doesn't matter which spouse) to continue to get health insurance from the employee spouse's company, provided that company has at least 20 employees, for three years after the divorce. Smaller group health insurance plans often are covered by COBRA laws as well, but the benefits may not extend as long.

The health insurance company is not obligated to offer someone who is covered by COBRA the discounted, subsidized group rate but will charge the full rate. If any premiums are missed, the insurance company does not have to reinstate you. It is important to shop for health insurance. Even though the COBRA provision may supply a quick solution to health care coverage, it may not be the best. Quality health insurance may be purchased at a lesser cost somewhere else.

At any age you'll soon want to explore other options. If you can match the rate from your spouse's company or get a lower premium with another company, buy your own, don't continue COBRA. Then if something happens, you are covered as long as you pay your premiums. Otherwise, at the end of three years, COBRA drops you, and then you have to start shopping again. By that time, you might be uninsurable and not able to find insurance. Special rules apply to governmental plans because they are not covered by COBRA.

Most states have insurance for those who are uninsurable and cannot get health insurance any other way. As may be expected, this insurance is very costly. It is better to look ahead and get individual health insurance for a lower premium while you are healthy than to gamble that you will still be healthy three years later.

Is health insurance a marital asset? Maybe. Some companies provide health benefits for employees after they retire. Some lawyers are starting to consider this an asset ever since the Financial Accounting Standards Board in 1993 began requiring employers to calculate the present value of the future benefits and show a liability for that value in their financial reports.

▶ Insurance to Protect Spousal Support for Farther Down the Road

Even though the divorce decree stipulates one spouse is to pay the other a certain amount of maintenance for a certain period of time, that doesn't mean it will happen. Several things can happen to the payer that can cause payments to stop or decrease. Fortunately, there are ways to guard against this and ensure that payments will be made. These include life insurance, disability insurance, and annuities; we call them "air bags" because they protect you later on down the road.

An Alimony "Air Bag": Life Insurance

Alimony payments stop upon the death of the payer. One simple way to cover future payments is to have your divorce decree stipulate that life insurance will be carried on the life of the payer to replace alimony in the event of the payer's death.

If you are the spouse who will receive alimony or any other payments, we recommend that *you* own the life insurance policy and whether or not your ex will be required to make the premium payments according to the divorce decree. This prevents any changes in the policy without your knowledge. For example, consider what happened to Joan. She was receiving $400 per month in alimony from her ex-husband Jerry. The court had ordered Jerry to carry life insurance on his life, payable to Joan as long as alimony was being paid. After three years, Jerry was tired of making the insurance payments so he stopped and the insurance was canceled. Nobody knew about it until one year later. Jerry was in a car accident and died two weeks later of complications from his injuries. Alimony came to an abrupt halt and there was no life insurance! Yes, Jerry was in contempt of court, but it didn't make any difference.

Hazard!

Be an Owner!

The recipient spouse should either own the life insurance or be an irrevocable beneficiary for three reasons:

1. to make sure the premiums are paid,
2. to receive tax-favored treatment, and
3. to make sure the beneficiary is not changed.

The type of insurance you purchase may depend on your cash flow. You could select a *whole life policy* that accumulates cash value over time, or a *term policy,* which will cost less, for the life of the alimony owed. It is a term need, therefore term life insurance will generally be the best vehicle to use to guarantee full payment.

Hazard!

Bridge Out Ahead?

If you need new insurance, you should apply for it before your divorce is final. If the spouse paying the alimony cannot pass the physical and purchase new insurance, there is still time to modify the final settlement to make up for this possibility.

If the court orders a spouse to purchase insurance to cover alimony, child support, or both, and that spouse owns the policy, the premium payments are treated like alimony for tax purposes and can be deducted from taxable income. Likewise, the spouse who is the beneficiary of the policy will need to declare the paid premiums as taxable income.

Another Air Bag: Disability Insurance

A second way to protect the stream of alimony income is to have disability insurance on the payer's ability to earn income. Assume, for example, that you pay your ex $1,200 per month based on your salary of $6,000 per month. Then, you become disabled. If you had disability insurance, you might then be able to receive $4,000 per month tax-free and could continue making maintenance payments. If you had no insurance and no income, you would probably go back to court and ask to have alimony reduced.

You must own your own disability policy. Your ex may make the payments on it so that there is a guarantee that it stays in force (at least, as long as the premiums are paid).

A Third "Air Bag": The Annuity

A third way to protect alimony is to have the spouse who is paying alimony buy an annuity that pays a certain amount per month that equals the alimony payment. To do this, the spouse paying alimony needs to make a large lump-sum deposit to an annuity with an insurance company and instruct it to make the specific payment. The annuity in turn will send a monthly check. Once the alimony obligation has been met, payment will revert to the spouse who has been paying.

Here's an important issue—once an annuity is annuitized (meaning regular payments are being made), it is irrevocable; it can't be canceled, nor can you receive the original lump sum back. If you are the recipient you need not worry about receiving your monthly support payment.

▶ Traveling with Kids: What You Need to Know About Child Support

There are many issues related to child support, including the decision regarding custody (sole vs. split vs. joint), and all of the arrangements that must be made in support of whichever custodial decision you and your partner make. This section, however, focuses on the financial issues, as that's the purpose of this book.

Every parent is obligated to support their children, regardless of divorce. In a divorce situation, the noncustodial parent usually is ordered to pay some child support to the custodial parent. The remainder of the child's expenses is paid by the custodial parent.

What's the Toll? Determining the Amount of Child Support Payments

All states now have child support guidelines that help the courts decide the amount of child support to be paid. The support obligation of each parent is often based on the ratio of each parent's income, the percentage of time the child spends with each parent, the amount of alimony paid to the custodial parent, and historic child-related expenses.

Hazard!

Every parent is obligated to support his or her children, regardless of divorce. In a divorce, the noncustodial parent is usually ordered to pay some child support to the custodial parent. The remainder of the children's expenses is paid by the custodial parent.

To see what you might be paying (or receiving) in child support, let's consider the example of Paul and Becky. They have two kids. Their joint gross income is $5,200 a month. Paul's is $4,300, Becky's is $900 a month:

Paul	$4,300	83%
Becky	900	17%
	$5,200	100%

Paul is earning 83 percent of the total and Becky is earning 17 percent. In their state, the child support guidelines for spouses with a gross income of $5,200 and two children is $983. According to the state guidelines, if Paul pays *no alimony,* he will be obligated to pay Becky $813 in monthly child support—83 percent of the suggested monthly payment of $983.

However, what if Paul also pays alimony of $1,000 per month? At this point, sharpen your pencil, and subtract the $1,000 from his income and add it to hers.

Paul	$4,300	−	$1,000	=	$3,300	63%
Becky	900	+	1,000	=	1,900	37
	$5,200				$5,200	100%

As you can see, the totals stay the same, but the percentages change. Now, Paul's percentage is 63 percent of the total gross monthly income. Using the same guidelines formula, multiply $983 by 63 percent. Because Paul also pays alimony to Becky, his child support is reduced to $624 per month.

Paul and Becky present a very simplistic example. Other factors may enter in—for example, who pays for child care, health insurance, or education or school expenses? If it's Paul, then it would be necessary to adjust the amount of child support he pays. In other cases, if custody is split, then the numbers get altered quite a bit. Keep in mind that you and your soon-to-be-ex should discuss not only child support, but college costs, insurance, estate planning documents, school tuition, summer camp or other vacation activities, orthodontia or other major medical and dental costs not reimbursed by insurance, and other possible expenses for your children.

Hazard!
Balancing Act

The rule of thumb is that as alimony increases, child support decreases.

The bottom line is that the guidelines are only *guidelines*. The key factors will depend on your personal and financial situation. It is not unusual for the amount of child support paid to be less than the actual amount realistically required to meet the needs of growing children. And many times, the child support is not paid at all. The payer of child support may harbor suspicion or anger against the custodial parent. The payer may think that the custodial parent is spending the money on personal stuff—not on the kids.

Be realistic. Child support is based on income. And it is based on the lifestyle that was already established—when both parents were under the same roof. In an ideal world (although the ideal is a myth, in most cases), the payer should think, "I want my kids to live in this kind of a house. I have to pay enough support that will make that kind of house payment possible. That means my ex is going to be there, too."

If the Road Ahead Changes: Modifying Child Support

What happens when circumstances change after your divorce is final—say, one of you loses your job or becomes disabled or a settlement or judgment (not related to your divorce) is awarded that was started when you were still married, or if one of you wins the lottery?

Child support is usually modified for a substantial change in circumstances. How much of a change constitutes a "substantial" change in circumstance? Obviously, if income changes, it would change the child support according to the child support guidelines.

Suppose you have two children and child support is agreed on. At some point, your older child decides to go live with Dad in the summertime. Because Dad is paying the full cost of supporting this child at his house (at least for several months), Dad thinks, "Now, I only have to pay half the child support," and he sends a check for half the amount. Because it was not changed

Hazard!

Changing the Route to Child Support

Your property settlement is final, and you and your spouse usually cannot change anything about the property settlement unless you can prove fraud. However, child support is different: it can be modified.

by a court order, he still owes the whole amount and the ex-wife could force him to pay that back child support he did not pay.

Or, suppose that both kids go to live with Dad during the summer. He thinks, "I don't have to pay any child support during the summer, because both kids are living with me." Right? Wrong. The court order says that he must pay so much every month. It does not say "nine months out of the year." Unless the court order specifies nonpayments during certain months, the spouse paying child support is liable for those payments, and the ex-spouse could sue for that money. Again, consult your attorney for guidelines on custody criteria and child support in your state.

Hazard!

It is important for you and your ex-spouse to have all child support agreements in writing, because your circumstances may change.

The Big Toll: Income Tax Considerations

Child support payments aren't deductible—ever. They are never included in the recipient's taxable income.

If you have only one child, the child can be counted as an exemption by only one parent in a given year. Unless otherwise specified, the exemption usually goes to the parent who has physical custody of the child for the greater portion of the calendar year.

The exemption can be traded back and forth year to year between parents, with a written waiver or IRS Form 8332. Once the custodial parent has executed the waiver, the noncustodial parent must attach the form to the income tax return. If the waiver is for more than one year, it must be attached each year.

If you have two or more children, you and your ex-spouse can divide up the exemptions, if you agree. The children's Social Security numbers must be listed on each parent's tax return.

For either parent to claim the exemption, the child must be in the custody of at least one parent for more than one-half of the calendar year. And if the child lives with a grandparent or someone other than a parent for more than one-half of the calendar year, neither parent can claim the exemption.

Hazard!

Divorced parents who claim the same children on their tax returns are inviting an IRS audit.

Child Care Credits. A custodial parent who pays child care expenses so that they can be gainfully employed may be eligible for a tax credit. To claim this credit, the parent must maintain a household that is the home of at least one child, and the day care expenses must be paid to someone who is not claimed as a dependent. Caution here. Our tax laws change, and so does the amount allocated for child care. Make sure you check with your accountant or financial adviser as to what is currently allowed.

Only the custodial parent is entitled to claim both the child and the dependent care credit. This is true even if the custodial parent does not claim the dependency exemption for the child. A noncustodial parent may *not* claim a child care credit for expenses incurred, even if that parent is entitled to claim the exemption for the child.

Here's an example. Carl and Mandy's son Bret, age 4, lives with Mandy four days a week and with Carl three days a week. Both Carl and Mandy work outside the home and each pays one-half of the $5,000 per year that it costs to have Bret in day care during the work week. Mandy gets to claim a child care credit for her share of the day care expenses. Although Carl and Mandy each have custody of Bret for a significant portion of the week, Mandy is considered the custodial parent because Bret spends a greater percentage of time with her than he does with Carl.

Head of the Household. A head-of-household filing status is available to any-one (divorced or single) who provides more than one-half the cost of main-taining the household, and who provides the primary home of at least one qualifying person for more than one-half of the year. A "qualifying person" is the taxpayer's child or any other person who qualifies as a dependent.

In determining whether the home is the principal home of the child for more than one-half of the year, do not count absences for vacation, sickness, school, or military service as time spent away from home if it is reasonable to assume that the child will return to the home.

If You Have to Make a U-Turn: Going Back to Court to Enforce Child Support

The court that dissolves your marriage will keep jurisdiction over you and your ex and any children, so that any orders or judgments can be enforced. Child support is the most common example of an order that is violated. If the required payments have not been made, then there are a number of methods that can be used to force the payments: garnishment of pay, seizing bank accounts or property, and imprisonment. There are even newspapers that publish a "most wanted" deadbeat parents list, including photos of parents who don't pay child support.

Route 1: Garnishing Wages. Enforcement of orders for child support and alimony can be made through a process commonly referred to as *garnish-ment.* This legal action is also called a *wage assignment, income withhold-ing order,* or *income deduction order.* This is an order that is directed to the employer of the paying parent, requiring the employer to divert a portion of the employee's salary to the ex-spouse who is due the payment. This is a common process and should be understood by any attorney who does even a few divorce cases.

Many attorneys are surprised to learn that the salary or retirement pay of a federal employee or retiree can be easily garnished for alimony or child support. Also, attorney fees and court costs can be added to the amount taken out of the pay.

In some states, a garnishment order is done automatically as part of the initial court order process. In other states, the action is brought at a later time when there is a problem in missed or late payments. In the states where it is done automatically, the garnishment automatically goes into effect if the supporting parent falls behind for a certain number of days. After that, the

Roadmap 4.1

13 Things to Know About Money and Divorce

1. In general, the longer you and your spouse were married, the longer alimony will be paid.

2. It is possible for a husband to get alimony.

3. The amount and length of alimony depends on factors such as the length of your marriage, the needs of the spouse who will receive alimony, the ability of the other spouse to pay alimony, the previous lifestyle of both you and your spouse, and the age and health of both of you.

4. Sometimes alimony is paid so that one spouse can obtain a degree or update job skills.

5. Most alimony is not paid on a permanent basis.

6. If properly structured, alimony will be *taxable* to the recipient and *deductible* by the payer.

7. Child support, however, is *not deductible* by the party who pays it and is not income (and therefore *not taxable*) to the parent who has custody of the child.

8. Because alimony payments will stop if the paying spouse dies, if you are receiving alimony, consider purchasing life insurance on your ex-spouse to protect the alimony income stream.

9. Alimony should not change or end within six months of any child's 18th, or 21st birthday, or age of emancipation in that particular state.

10. If you are to be the beneficiary of life insurance, you should own the policy and pay the premiums.

11. The amount of child support depends on a number of factors, the most important of which is the income of each parent.

12. In most states, a parent is not legally obligated to pay for a child's college education. Ask your attorney.

13. Depending on the employer, health care insurance coverage may be continued for the nonemployee after the couple divorces.

current support and arrearages are automatically deducted until back payments are made up or there is a court order stopping the action.

Route 2: Using a "Friend of the Court." Many states now provide for support enforcement at no charge through an office sometimes called the "friend of the court." In these programs, the payments are sent directly to the court clerk, who records the payments and then sends them on to the recipient. The transactions are computerized and therefore it is easier to track arrearages and late payments.

In jurisdictions that have this setup, it is customary for the attorney representing the spouse who is to be paid to ask for a court order requiring payments through the clerk's office. And sometimes this method is also better for the paying spouse, because there will be a good history of compliance with the court order. This system means that the receiving spouse will not be able to claim that the check was late or did not get there at all.

You may also be interested to know that nonsupport actions can also be brought in your local criminal court. You will have to weigh the likelihood of recovery through collection action alone before you decide to start a criminal prosecution. In addition, many states have laws that track deadbeat parents and keep them from getting driver's licenses or professional licenses and that seize tax refund checks.

E-Z Pass

How to Make it Through Your Divorce without Going Broke

As soon as the subject of divorce comes up, your financial well-being is at risk. This chapter describes several steps you can take to maintain some control over the situation. Whether—and when—you take all of the steps depends on how your household finances are organized, the possibility that your spouse may be taking some of the actions described in this chapter, and the likelihood that your spouse will follow through with divorce proceedings. Nevertheless, it's critical that you know your financial rights during and after divorce. This chapter focuses on how much money you'll have during and after your divorce.

▶ Driving Solo: Coming to Terms with Your Financial Situation

One of the great myths of separating and divorcing couples is that it is cheaper to live as a single than as a couple. Here's the fallacy in that thinking: right now, you *both* contribute to your lifestyle. And if you're like many couples, you struggle each month to make the paychecks stretch to pay the bills.

Hazard!

Be Aware of the Financial Pitfalls of Divorce

1. You may not be able to keep the house.
2. You may need to share your pension.
3. In divvying up household items, you may not be able to keep your favorite things.
4. You may not have as much money as you want, need, or used to have.

If you can barely live on your *combined* incomes before you divorce, how do you think you can continue to live at the *same* standard after divorcing and setting up two households—one for you and one for your ex? After the divorce, expenses that you didn't think about begin to surface. Tollbooth 5.1 lists some of these additional expenses—both small and big.

Most women and men feel they've been taken to the cleaners when the divorce is finally over. They did not consider these "extra expenses" when negotiating a settlement. The first thing that most do is to liquidate some of the assets received in the divorce settlement to pay for the extra expenses. No wonder everyone feels they got cheated.

Tollbooth 5.1

Expenses for Two Households

▶ Two house payments (or rent payments)
▶ Two utility bills (one for each house)
▶ Two telephone bills (one for each house)
▶ New furniture for the second home
▶ Kitchen staples (basic foods, cleaning supplies) and utensils (pots, pans, dishes)
▶ Automotive maintenance and repairs
▶ Convenience foods (New singles spend more money on take-out, eating out, and fast food.)
▶ Kid's expenses (You may want to double up on many things so that your kids have belongings at Mom's *and* Dad's.)

Estimating New Tolls: Consider Your Standard of Living

Most likely, you won't be able to maintain your previous standard of living after the divorce, so be ready to adjust your budget accordingly. Make sure the financial projections for your budget consider the impact of inflation over time. If not, you may underestimate the share of property you will need to maintain your agreed-upon lifestyle.

Hire a Professional "Driver": Visit a Financial Advisor Specializing in Divorce

As part of your divorce team strongly consider a financial professional who specializes in helping divorcing parties achieve an equitable financial settlement.

You may want your attorney to actually contract with the financial professional, because this may extend attorney-client privilege to conversations, memos, and work products of the financial professional. Make sure that your financial professional has the knowledge and skills specific to the financial aspects of divorce—for example, they have earned the Certified Divorce Financial Analyst credential, administered by the Institute for Divorce Financial Analysts (see Appendix B for contact information).

▶ Get a New Air Bag: Make Sure You Still Have Health Insurance

Don't overlook the cost of health insurance after a divorce, and do factor it into your budget. Once your divorce is final, you're no longer covered under your ex-spouse's health insurance plan.

If you are not employed, or if you don't have insurance through your employer, one option is COBRA. The federal law that says an ex-spouse (you) is entitled to health insurance coverage through COBRA for 36 months from the time a divorce is finalized (as discussed in Chapter 4). Since you must pay the premium, this may be expensive. You also need to be in a position to have replacement insurance before the 36 months expires. Note: A qualified beneficiary must notify the plan administrator of a qualifying event within 60 days of the divorce or legal separation.

▶ On the Road with Uncle Sam: Getting Social Security Benefits from Your Ex-Spouse

You're also entitled to Social Security benefits based on the earnings of your ex-spouse, if the following is true:

- ▶ The higher-earning ex-spouse is entitled to receive Social Security benefits.
- ▶ You were married for 10 years or more before your divorce became final.
- ▶ The lower-earning ex-spouse is not married.
- ▶ The lower-earning ex-spouse is age 62 or over.
- ▶ The lower-earning ex-spouse is not entitled to a Social Security retirement benefit that equals or exceeds one-half of the higher-earning ex-spouse's benefit.

The higher-earning ex-spouse doesn't have to be retired, either, for the lower-earning ex-spouse to begin receiving retirement benefits. For more information, refer back to Chapter 3, which covered Social Security benefits in detail in terms of pension-related benefits; also see Appendix B.

▶ Take the Low Road: Learn How to Reduce Your Expenses

So, where does this leave you? Remember the sleuthing you were doing digging up papers and information for your attorney to fill out the various forms you file during the divorce? (If not, refer back to Chapter 2.) Your hard work will come in handy here.

You'll also need to take a hard look at what you consider necessary expenses. If you are accustomed to taking a fabulous vacation each year, you probably feel that it should be part of your regular life style postdivorce. That's not necessarily so. Spending the day golfing or lounging by the country club pool may not be in the cards, either. Also, if your normal expenses include $350 per month for clothes and you have two closets' full, you may need to make them last longer than before.

Typically, divorce changes everybody's life. To determine your minimum financial needs, ask yourself the following:

- ▶ Will I have enough to support my current lifestyle?
- ▶ Will I be able to keep the assets from our division of marital assets without having to deplete them to pay living expenses?
- ▶ Will I be able to contribute to savings and retirement funds as I need to?

If any of the answers are "no," you will have to look seriously at your budget and adjust your standard of living. It has been proven that most of us can easily live on at least 10 percent less than we currently do.

Consider the following examples of two women, Sally and Jean, who both went through divorces, but with very different financial outcomes. Sally and Jean had been best friends since growing up in a small Midwestern town. Both their fathers worked at a local factory, and there never seemed to be enough money to go around in either family. In college, Sally met and married Don, whose career skyrocketed. She became active in her community, chairing fundraisers for charitable events and participating in several clubs. They moved to a mansion complete with two maids, and, later, two children. It seemed like an ideal life.

Jean, on the other hand, married Stan, who worked at the factory where her father worked. Like Sally, Jean had two children. She became skilled at sewing their clothes and making good, budget-conscious meals.

As time went by, with the children were grown and on their own, both couples decided to divorce. Sally was accustomed to living on an "allowance" of $138,000 per year, whereas Jean could do well on $21,000 per year. Sally's husband Don argued that her best friend, Jean, could live on $21,000 per year—so why couldn't she?

Sally didn't see how she could possibly cut her budget to less than $92,000 per year. When Sally's divorce was final, Don agreed to pay her alimony of $60,000 per year for six years, the $850,000 house, and $262,000, half of his retirement account.

After the divorce was final, Sally continued to spend $92,000 per year. She retained her membership in the country club and continued as the chair of their annual fund drive. She felt it was important to keep up her image as a successful, dynamic woman doing volunteer work within the community. She knew that there was a shortfall between the alimony she received and the actual amount she spent each year. She also knew that she could tap into the retirement account to cover any shortages, and she did.

No one initially told her that the money she withdrew from the retirement account would be both taxed and penalized for early withdrawal. Although once she was aware of it, that didn't stop her either. After all, she had her image to keep up. Within six years, the retirement account was depleted. On top of that, her alimony payments of $60,000 came to a screeching halt. Her only asset was her $850,000 house, which certainly was not a measly amount of money! But, with Sally's track record, whatever equity she had accumulated would be gone within a few years at her spending pace.

She had no paying job, no income from alimony, and no retirement fund. Just the house. She cried to her friend Jean, "If I had only known how fast my money would disappear, I would have spent more carefully or gotten a job or something!"

And how did Jean fare during this same time? Stan paid her half his salary, $19,000, for five years, and half his retirement account. She earned another $7,500 per year from a part-time job. With her sewing skills and ability to get along well with few resources, she was able to add $5,000 per year to her mutual fund and retirement accounts that totaled $22,000 when her divorce was final. In the same six years while Sally was going broke on $60,000 per year, Jean's mutual funds and retirement accounts had grown to $81,135.

Don't Crash and Burn: What Sally Did Wrong After Her Divorce

Choice is an important word for most people today. Sally had plenty of them, but she made bad choices:

▶ She chose not to work for pay. With her country club connections, she could have tapped into a well-paying job from someone who knew of her organizational and fund-raising skills. Or, if her pride wouldn't let her ask her friends for job leads, she certainly could have gotten some training and coaching from a career counselor to secure a position.

▶ She chose to keep the $850,000 home, which was free and clear of a mortgage. She felt she had an image to keep up and couldn't make do with a more modest house. She chose to sit on an asset that was not liquid and did not produce any income for her. If she had decided to buy a smaller home at half the cost of her current home and invest the difference, she could have realized an extra $36,000 per year in interest income at 8 percent.

▶ She chose not to reduce her expenses. Large homes cost money. Hers required the use of caretakers, which included a maid, housekeeper, and gardener.

- She chose to continue to buy clothes at the rate of $1,000 per month. It didn't matter that she had four closets' full already. But she didn't want to be seen in the same thing over and over.
- She chose to continue to have lavish parties and entertain on a large scale. Her image was more important today than how she would look tomorrow. "What will people think if I don't stay visible in the community?" she asked.
- She chose to continue to travel for relaxation and leisure. "I have to get away once in a while to recuperate," she said.
- She chose to have her hair, nails, and facials done weekly. "After all," she said, "I must look my best."

▶ Prepare for Your Post-Divorce Journey: Prevent Financial Misery

This whole chapter is about evaluating your expenses. It is important to make reasonable decisions when facing divorce. Are you willing to change your spending patterns and live at a reduced lifestyle in return for not having to live with your spouse anymore? This is a critical question. It doesn't necessarily make sense to trade one kind of misery (emotional—assuming you're the spouse seeking the divorce) for another kind (financial). And, of course, you may not have a choice. In either case, you don't have to live in financial misery after divorce if you can:

- negotiate a reasonable settlement;
- adjust your spending patterns so you don't tap into your assets, however minuscule they look; and
- take responsibility for some of the financial issues (this may mean getting a better job, or even just any job).

Share the Driving Burden: Be Open with Your Children

If you have kids, tell them the truth and let them help. Parents often hate to deprive their children of the designer jeans and shoes they have been getting. Instead, they go without other necessities to avoid letting their kids know the extent of the financial situation. This is insanity.

Experience shows that when kids are part of the financial decision-making and are privy to the income and expenses of the household, wondrous things can happen. The "gimmes" that are so prevalent, especially when parents attempt to soften the emotional blow of divorce by buying things, almost vanish. Your kids can be incredible troupers at wanting to help cut costs and make things work. It becomes a game for them.

For example, one woman and her teenaged daughter became closer after the parents divorced because the mother was open about her financial situation. After the divorce, Marie lived with her mom during the summers and with her dad the rest of the year in another state. Carol was ashamed of how little money her job was paying. In desperation, she had no choice but to share her financial situation with her daughter. She just couldn't afford all the teenage things Marie wanted.

But what Carol thought was an embarrassment turned into an adventure. Carol would come home from work and find that Marie had found a bargain at the grocery store and had whipped up dinner for just a few dollars. Marie was so proud the day she found a bookcase at a garage sale that she knew her mother needed. All summer long, they found bargains and were able to laugh at their creativity.

Contrast that with the situation with another woman, Stella and her son, Josh. Stella was too proud to share her financial situation with Josh. When she grew up, her family didn't talk about money—it was not the proper thing to do. The end result was that she and Josh would argue over every purchase he wanted to make, creating a real strain in their relationship. He was convinced that his mother was a real miser and didn't care about his wants and needs. Or Stella would give in and buy the designer clothes for him instead of paying her credit card bill. Her money woes only deepened, and her relationship with Josh worsened.

Whose shoes would you rather be in: Stella's or Carol's? The choice is yours.

Pull Over: If You Don't Own It Now, Don't Buy It

Here's another case study to consider when preparing your finances for a divorce. Darrell and Laurie argued all the time about money. When they decided to get divorced, they made an effort to stay out of the war zones and make sensible decisions to make it as easy as possible through a trying time.

One day when Laurie got home from work, Darrell was unpacking a new computer. Laurie blasted at him about his irresponsible spending habits

—he had just spent the money they were going to use to pay to the attorney. Darrell tried to defend himself by explaining that he was expecting to learn new computer skills that would help him earn enough to ease their financial situation and, besides, he felt he deserved the computer to help him through this emotionally difficult time.

Needless to say, with this additional financial burden, Laurie became so angry that their efforts to have a friendly divorce were sabotaged.

While you're going through your divorce it is not the time to buy a new house or a new car or add any new debts. This is also not the time to invest in any product or to shift investment assets. Investments that you make during this time could have enormous financial strings attached, including Uncle Sam's. Your property may be divided in a different way than you thought it would be. There will be costs to split it up, and possibly penalties in shifting assets from one spouse to the other.

Unless the property division has already been decided before purchase, how do you know who is going to get which asset? Shifting assets could create difficulty in tracking the location and ownership of the asset, and a suspicion that someone is hiding assets.

Don't Drive Recklessly: Beware of Raiding Bank Accounts

This is also a tricky area. There is a balance between having enough to live on and taking money just to be vindictive. Then there is the situation where you may just want to make sure you get what is rightfully yours before it disappears.

Take Molly. Her husband, Daniel, walked out after years of bitter fighting. He was the breadwinner and she stayed home and raised their four kids. Before he left, he gave her money each month for bills and groceries. After he left, she didn't hear from him, nor did he leave any money for her. She did hear from the bank. Nothing had been paid on the car or mortgage. She borrowed from friends to feed the kids until she could borrow no more.

Molly knew it was time to hire an attorney. The first three attorneys she called wouldn't take her case because she had no money to pay a retainer. The moral here is that it would have been prudent for her to have taken money from their bank account immediately after Daniel left home to allow for such emergencies.

Hazard!

Protect Yourself, but Don't Be Greedy

If you decide to withdraw money, be reasonable. You should not take more than half from any account!

Then there's the opposite. Consider the case of Patricia and Ken. When Ken left, Patricia was so angry that she went to their bank and raided their accounts. She depleted them and moved the money to a different bank in a different city. Now, Ken had a hard time making ends meet when he needed cash. That point was brought out strongly in their court trial, which prejudiced the judge against Patricia.

▶ Paying Tolls Down the Road: Common Credit Card Dilemmas

So how can you pay for your new, separate life? An increasing number of divorcing couples are showing up with large amounts of debt, mostly credit card debt. If it's true that misery loves company, and you too are over your head in debt, then the good news is that you are not alone.

Take the High Road: Be Smart When You Use Credit

It's tempting to overcharge. If you're like most people, your mailbox is packed with credit card applications offering a very low percentage rate, even zero percent interest for a six-month period on outstanding balances. Who can resist? It looks like free money, right?

The problem is that this low-interest charge prompts even more spending, and six months later, with an even larger credit balance, the interest rate jumps up to somewhere between 14 percent and 20 percent. Now you're in trouble! You have to stretch just to make the minimum payments. Suddenly you realize you're living beyond your means. You'll be paying for that sweater or new CD unit you couldn't afford yesterday—but charged anyway —for many tomorrows to come.

It's tempting to start living off your credit cards when the spouse who moves out stops sending money. If there is absolutely no money, it may be necessary to use credit cards, but *do so sparingly*. It is more important to pare down your living expenses to the bare bone. This means no vacation, no new clothes, even no home or car improvements—unless you have the cash to pay for it.

As in most cases, there seems to be another side. Some attorneys advise their clients to buy whatever they need and run up the credit card balance. Why? Because it's considered marital debt and your soon-to-be-ex will have to pay for half of it. *This is bad advice.* Too many times spouses max out the credit cards before the divorce. After the divorce, each spouse has difficulty paying off their share or getting any other type of credit. Once you run into trouble making credit card payments, you have put your credit standing into jeopardy. It just isn't worth it.

Most couples also don't discuss openly what their financial situation is and who is to take responsibility for paying the bills after the divorce is final. Without properly notifying the creditors of the divorce and canceling open joint credit cards, both spouses are liable for the debts. Creditors must be notified and must authorize any agreement drawn to release and remove the spouse who will not be responsible for the payment.

Problems with credit cards after divorce can come back to haunt you if you don't take the proper steps to release yourself from the liability.

Avoid Detours: Protect Your Credit

There are several actions you should take after your divorce to protect your credit.

Check Your Credit Report. Make sure you are aware of all requests for credit, purchases, or loans. Continue to monitor your credit history status on at least an annual basis to ensure that there's no incorrect information or unlawful activity by someone else.

Notify Creditors of Your Situation. Cancel joint credit accounts. Remove your name from the accounts, or have your spouse's name removed from the account if it will be your responsibility. For accounts that must be in both your names (utilities, mortgage, and the like), contact the creditor and ask to be notified directly if a payment is missed.

Establish Credit in Your Name Alone. If you haven't already done so, establish credit in your own name right away. That will help you build the good personal credit history you'll need to make major purchases, rent an apartment, or buy a new home.

Open an Individual Bank Account. Move an appropriate amount of your joint funds into your new personal account to prevent your spouse from withdrawing all of your funds without your knowledge.

Get Copies of Your Past Income Tax Returns. You will need copies for at least the last five years. Put them in a safe place. Also, get copies of other key financial information such as loan agreements, bank statements, brokerage statements, and creditor statements.

Roadblock #1: What to Do if Your Ex-Spouse Ruined Your Credit

Sometimes, one person in a marriage may ruin the credit of both and you would feel that pinch even after the divorce. Many people are even scared to see what their credit report says about them. Don't panic! Not seeing your credit report prevents you from deleting any inaccuracies that are being reported.

Many times one spouse—for example, a wife, though the situation could also be true of a husband—will have less information on her credit report than her husband, because she was not the originator of the line of credit, or the line of credit is only in the husband's name.

Your report may not be as bad as you think. Request credit reports from all three credit reporting bureaus (Appendix B provides contact information). Review each report and dispute with the credit reporting agency any incorrect, inaccurate, or erroneous information that appears on it. The credit reporting agency must investigate your dispute with the creditor and remove any items that are not correct or verifiable by the creditor. (Again, see Appendix B for information on credit reporting agencies.)

If there is debt information on your credit report that is your spouse's responsibility, contact the credit reporting agency and notify the creditor.

Keep in mind, though, that if your ex-spouse overextended the credit and fell behind in making payments, you may be responsible for those payments, even after your divorce. In a community property state, both husband and wife are responsible for repayment of the debts. Credit cards and loans that are in one person's name alone will affect only that person's credit rating. But if your name is listed on any debts, the credit card companies report the payment history on your credit report.

Roadblock #2: What to Do If Your Spouse Stops Making Credit Payments

Some divorce decrees require one spouse to make payments on the credit cards that the couple held jointly. If your spouse later quits making the payments, those creditors may come after you, and, again, your good credit may be jeopardized. To prevent this situation, you need to know more about joint credit.

Unfortunately, most couples who divorce have the misconception that they are *released* from any credit obligation for payments if the judge orders either the husband or wife to be solely responsible for making a specific payment. However, when you apply for credit *jointly,* you *both* are responsible for the repayment of the debt. If your spouse was ordered to make the payments on the debt owed and doesn't pay, the creditors legally can pursue you for payment. The creditor will continue to report all payment history on both of you as long as the account is open and held jointly.

If this happens to you, you should contact the creditor and explain your situation. Ask the creditor to release you from the liability of this debt and remove your name from the account. Your ex-spouse must be in agreement with this and should support this agreement with a letter to the creditor. The letter must include a statement from your ex-spouse taking full responsibility for the payments. Should the creditor agree to do this, you will no longer be responsible for the account. Your name will be removed from the account. All payment and credit history on that account will stop being reported on your credit report.

Roadblock #3: What to Do If Your Ex-Spouse Continues to Use a Joint Line of Credit or Credit Cards

After their divorce, some people unfortunately discover that their ex-spouses are still using the line of credit or charge cards that they had held jointly during the marriage. To prevent this, you should know that unless you specifically addressed the disbursements of your credit card accounts in your divorce, your ex-spouse can still use the credit cards. Obviously this is the *wrong* thing to do because you are still *jointly* responsible for making the payments, no matter who made the new purchase.

Therefore, it is important to know which of you will be responsible for the account. You can call the credit card company to find out if you or your ex-spouse was the primary applicant. You also can check your credit reports to see which of the accounts listed reflect the accounts as joint, individual, or a user card. Depending on how the account was set up, there are different ways to handle this credit problem:

▶ If your accounts were taken out in your ex-spouse's name and you are a *user* of the account, contact the creditor and request the removal of your name from the account.

▶ If an account is a *joint* account, you need to notify the credit card company immediately requesting your name be removed from the account and stating that you have no liability for any activity since the divorce.

▶ If you were the *primary applicant* for the credit card, you can request in writing that the account be closed. This would stop new activity on the account. Your ex-spouse should agree to make the payments because they are for the purchases you didn't make. However if your ex-spouse doesn't make payments, you still can be held liable for payment because you were the primary applicant. Remember, unless you resolve these problems with your ex-spouse and take the appropriate action, the activity will continue to be reported on your credit report.

Roadblock #4: What to Do If the IRS Comes After You

If the IRS comes after you to collect taxes they say you owe, this will also show up on your credit report. Again, don't panic. Rather than be afraid to see your credit report, you need to face whatever problems you are having and resolve them. Fear is felt when you don't know what you are facing. By jumping in and facing your fears, you can make a plan and look for solutions more easily.

First, request a copy of your credit report from all three credit reporting agencies. Check to see if the IRS has filed any tax liens against you. Review any items on your credit report that are not accurate or not yours. Dispute each item on your credit report that is not accurate or is not yours by writing a letter to the credit reporting agencies.

If the money the IRS is indicating that you owe was from the years that you were married to your ex-spouse and they can't collect from your ex-spouse, they will try to collect from you. If you are in financial hardship, you can complete a financial statement showing the hardship. The IRS may allow you to make small payments, or if the hardship is great enough, they will put you in an uncollectible status.

If, on the other hand, the money the IRS is trying to collect from you is for taxes owed by your ex-spouse *after* your divorce, you should see a tax attorney. You are *not* responsible for taxes from returns after your divorce that were not filed jointly.

▶ Looking Down the Road Ahead: Summing Up

It is very important to know what you spend money on and where you spend it. Determine which expenditures you can and you should trim. Don't make any financial commitments that you don't understand or are not absolutely clear about. Don't take out loans or add additional credit obligations on to your balance sheet. And, if you have kids, don't keep them in the dark. They have ESP and know all is not well. Game-playing doesn't deal a fair hand.

The Light at the End of the Tunnel

Post-Divorce Financial Planning

Now that you know what you got or will get from the division of assets, you can start planning for your post-divorce life. This planning phase involves money—*yours,* so it's especially important. You may have gotten a lump sum, you may receive it over a period of time, you may have to pay some out, or you may have none, at least right now. Even if you are in the latter situation, with no money to your name, *don't skip this chapter.* It's as much for you as for someone with deep pockets. In the previous chapter, we covered information you'll need on how to manage your *expenses and debt;* this chapter discusses how to put together a viable financial *savings and investing* plan for the next phase of your life, when you're traveling solo again.

▶ Hit the Road with a Revised Financial Plan

Let's start out with what might seem like the best-case scenario. Suppose you're getting a check from one of the joint accounts representing your portion of the divorce settlement. It may seem like a lot of money—a *huge* amount of money. You may be tempted to take that long-awaited vacation cruise, a reward for the stress and strain that you have been under. You may even think, "I might meet someone who *really* appreciates me!" But be careful: this is a dangerous road, with lots of curves ahead.

For example, consider the case of one woman who received a huge amount of money—and then spent it in just a few years, without doing any long-term financial planning.

Sharon should have done some better planning at the beginning. She blew it. With just a little planning, Sharon could have been set for life—$356,000 is a *lot* of money, money that could have given her a nice trip or two, but better still, it could have seeded multiple investments that would have created income and growth. A modern-day tragedy that is repeated way too often after the fallout of divorce. Your goal is not to repeat Sharon's misadventure. And the rest of this chapter can help.

What should be the first step in your post-divorce planning? Unless you are well-versed in the myriad choices available to you, start by talking to a financial planner, preferably a Certified Financial Planner. Roadmap 6.1 is a list of questions to ask a financial planner. This person can be your advisor

Dear Dad,

When I divorced Bob three years ago, I got a check for $356,000 in return for no alimony. I didn't tell you how much it was at the time, because I admit I didn't want you to tell me I should save it rather than spend it. I thought I had won the lottery—I had never seen so much money! Since then (as you know), I've traveled, bought jewelry and a new car, and given money to friends. I even took several friends to Europe with me. But I didn't buy a house or save or invest any money. I've had a wonderful time, but my money runs out next month—can you help me? I'm not asking for money from you and Mom: I just need some advice on finding a financial planner and getting back on my feet. Please.

Love, Sharon

11 Questions to Ask a Financial Advisor

1. **Do you have the CFP (Certified Financial Planner) or ChFC (Chartered Financial Consultant) designations?** These designations ensure that the financial advisor has had specialized training in the field of financial planning.

2. **Do you have specialized training in the area of divorce?** A CDFA (Certified Divorce Financial Analyst) is a financial professional who has had additional training in the specifics of the financial issues in divorce.

3. **Do you work alone, or in an office with other professionals such as financial planners, accountants, attorneys, etc.?** No one person can know all the aspects of financial issues, divorce and tax laws, retirement issues, etc. When they have other professionals to bounce ideas off of, you'll get better help and advice. In addition, solo practitioners form professional relationships with these tax, legal, pension, and institutional specialists.

4. **Can you give me the names of some of your clients?** Ask for referrals who have worked with the advisor for a minimum of three years. (The advisor would have to get permission, if he or she does not have it, to give you the names of clients; otherwise it would be a breach of the client's privacy.)

5. **Typically, how often do you meet and/or speak with clients?** You want to hear from your financial advisor more than once a year. You want someone who will explain the statements you get and review your portfolio with you once in a while to see if you are reaching your goals.

6. **How do you charge?** There are typically three ways of charging:

   ▶ *Fee only*–The advisor charges for the time spent with you and for his or her advice. The advisor does not make a commission on financial products that you buy (e.g., stocks, bonds, mutual funds, insurance). Another type of fee-only advisor charges a percentage of your account; he or she does not make commissions on trades and does not charge for time spent with you. Fee-only advisors have fewer inherent conflicts of interest because of the way in which they are compensated.

   ▶ *Commission only*–This advisor does not charge for his or her time or for a financial plan that the advisor prepares (many do not prepare in-depth financial plans). This advisor earns a commission on any investments that you make. These are typically in-house financial products. Commission-only advisors tend to be transaction oriented.

► *Fee plus commission*–Typically, this advisor doesn't charge for a first marketing appointment. If comprehensive work is done later, such as a full financial plan, the advisor will charge for time spent on that. In addition, the advisor will receive a commission on any product that you purchase through him or her. In return, the advisor should give you service.

7. **Have you made errors in advising clients in the past?** Everyone makes mistakes, including financial advisors. Anyone who says, "No, I've never made any errors" is lying. Use someone else. If the advisor admits that he or she has made mistakes, ask what the mistakes were and what the advisor learned. Then you be the judge.

8. **Have any complaints been filed against you?** You can check with the National Association of Securities Dealers (NASD–1735 K St., N.W., Washington, DC 20006; 202-778-8000; http://www.nasd.com) or the Securities and Exchange Commission (SEC–405 Fifth St., N.W., Washington, DC 20549; 202-942-7040; http://www.sec.gov) for securities complaints. However, only securities-commission compensated advisors are affiliated with the NASD. Therefore, fee-only advisors won't be listed. Most advisors are registered with their state; check with your state departments that cover those areas. (See Appendix B for additional contact information.) Note: Very few complaints end up on these lists; such checks are not definitive.

9. **Where do you get your financial advice?** A terrific question; one that will surprise them. Some rely solely on information generated from their company, others aggressively seek other sources. Find out where and what.

10. **What publications do you read on a regular basis?** Let's hope it's more than *Time* and *Newsweek*. Magazines such as *Money*, *Fortune*, and newspapers including the *Wall Street Journal* should head the list. Depending on which associations the advisor belongs to, a professional trade journal usually comes with those memberships.

11. **What professional associations do you belong to and how long have you been advising clients?** Active professionals should belong to associations that enhance their skills and education. You should hear names such as the International Association of Financial Planners or the Institute of Certified Financial Planners.

and your guide. Your planner will help you put together a plan that will help you reach your financial goals.

▶ Stop #1: Kick Your Tires by Reviewing Your Expenses and Budget

To begin reassessing your financial situation, you should revise your net worth, cash flow, and budget. Your expenses have likely or will likely need to change, too. You may now have expenses, such as alimony and child support, that you did not have to account for previously, or you may be receiving alimony and child support but postdivorce your income would have dropped dramatically. You must adjust your spending accordingly. Roadmap 6.2 can help you total up all your liabilities (or expenses).

If you relied totally on your ex-spouse's credit and earnings history during your marriage, you are probably experiencing difficulty now that the marriage has ended. Under the Equal Credit Opportunity Act (ECOA), lenders may not discriminate against you because you are divorced, but that doesn't mean they cannot reject your application if you have no credit history or independent sources of income.

If you have trouble finding a bank that will grant you an open-end line of credit, you might establish your creditworthiness by assuming a secured credit line. In this case, you deposit a certain amount of money, such as $500, and thereby receive a $500 credit line. Over time, as you pay your bills responsibly, you will qualify for an unsecured credit line.

▶ Stop #2: Know What to Pack by Reassessing Your Current Assets and Financial Goals

Once you've found a financial advisor (or if you've decided to go it alone), begin the financial planning process by taking stock of your assets and liabilities. You've already done this (during the early stages of your divorce process) when you evaluated your household properties, any investments you have, any cash in the bank, or other types of accounts, but now it's time to review those assets. Roadmap 6.3 can help you get a handle on your current assets.

Roadmap 6.2

Liabilities Worksheet

Liabilities	To Whom	Interest Rate %	Due Date	Amount Due $
1. Current Liabilities (monthly)				
Alimony		_____ %		$ _____
Bills				
Electric & Gas				
Home Contractor				
Oil Company				
Physician & Dentist				
Retail Stores				
Telephone				
Other				
Child Support				
Loans to Individuals				
Total Monthly Liabilities				$ _____
Total Annual Liabilities (multiply monthly by 12)				$ _____
2. Unpaid Taxes				
Income Taxes				
Federal		_____ %		$ _____
State				
City				
Capital Gains Taxes				
Federal				
State				
City				
Property Taxes				
Sales Taxes (locality)				
Social Security Taxes (self-employed)				
Total Unpaid Taxes				$ _____
3. Real Estate Liabilities				
Home #1				
First Mortgage		_____ %		$ _____
Second Mortgage				
Home Equity Loan				
Home #2				
First Mortgage				
Second Mortgage				
Home Equity Loan				
Rental Property				
First Mortgage				
Second Mortgage				
Total Real Estate Liabilities				$ _____

Roadmap 6.2 (continued)

Liabilities Worksheet

Liabilities	To Whom	Interest Rate %	Due Date	Amount Due $
4. Installment Liabilities				
Automobile Loans	_____	_____ %	_____	$ _____
Bank Loans for Bill Consolidation	_____	_____	_____	_____
Credit Cards	_____	_____	_____	_____
Education Loans	_____	_____	_____	_____
Equipment and Appliance Loans	_____	_____	_____	_____
Furniture Loans	_____	_____	_____	_____
Home Improvement Loans	_____	_____	_____	_____
Liability Judgments	_____	_____	_____	_____
Life Insurance Loans	_____	_____	_____	_____
Margin Loans Against Securities	_____	_____	_____	_____
Overdraft Bank Loans	_____	_____	_____	_____
Retirement Plan Loans	_____	_____	_____	_____
Total Installment Liabilities				$ _____
Total Liabilities				$ _____

After your divorce, you should also reset your financial goals. For example, you may have been saving money to buy a home but now find that goal no longer attainable. Instead, your highest priority may be to pay off bills or build your emergency reserve fund.

Ask yourself these questions:

▶ Do you need extra cash right now on a monthly basis to supplement your income?

▶ Do you need to use up some of your assets to pay off any debt?

▶ Do you want to buy a house, which will reposition liquid assets to an illiquid asset? (*Liquid* assets are those where you can get the money or cash

Roadmap 6.3

Assets Worksheet

Date _____

Assets	Date Purchased	Original $ Value/Cost	Current $ Value
1. Current Assets			
Bonuses or Commissions (due you)	_____	$_____	$_____
Certificates of Deposit	_____	_____	_____
	_____	_____	_____
Checking Accounts	_____	_____	_____
	_____	_____	_____
Credit Union Accounts	_____	_____	_____
Money-Market Accounts	_____	_____	_____
	_____	_____	_____
Savings Accounts	_____	_____	_____
	_____	_____	_____
Savings Bonds	_____	_____	_____
	_____	_____	_____
Tax Refunds (due you)	_____	_____	_____
Treasury Bills	_____	_____	_____
	_____	_____	_____
Total Current Assets		$_____	$_____
2. Securities			
Bonds (type of bond)			
_____	_____	$_____	$_____
_____	_____	_____	_____
_____	_____	_____	_____
_____	_____	_____	_____
Bond Mutual Funds			
_____	_____	_____	_____
_____	_____	_____	_____
Individual Stocks			
_____	_____	_____	_____
_____	_____	_____	_____
_____	_____	_____	_____
_____	_____	_____	_____
_____	_____	_____	_____
_____	_____	_____	_____
Stock Mutual Funds			
_____	_____	_____	_____
_____	_____	_____	_____
_____	_____	_____	_____
_____	_____	_____	_____
Futures	_____	_____	_____
Warrants and Options	_____	_____	_____
Total Securities		$_____	$_____

Assets	Date Purchased	Original $ Value/Cost	Current $ Value
3. Real Estate			
Mortgage Receivable (due you)	_____	$_____	$_____
Primary Residence	_____	_____	_____
Rental Property	_____	_____	_____
Real Estate Limited Partnerships	_____	_____	_____
Second Home	_____	_____	_____
Total Real Estate		$_____	$_____
4. Long-Term Assets			
Annuities	_____	$_____	$_____
IRAs	_____	_____	_____
Keogh Accounts	_____	_____	_____
Life Insurance Cash Values	_____	_____	_____
Loans Receivable (due you)	_____	_____	_____
Pensions	_____	_____	_____
Private Business Interests	_____	_____	_____
Profit-Sharing Plans	_____	_____	_____
Royalties	_____	_____	_____
Salary Reduction Plans (401(k), 403(b), 457 plans)	_____	_____	_____
Total Long-term Assets		$_____	$_____
5. Personal Property			
Antiques	_____	$_____	$_____
Appliances (washing machines, dishwashers, vacuum cleaners, etc.)	_____	_____	_____
Automobiles	_____	_____	_____
Boats, etc.	_____	_____	_____
Campers, Trailers, etc.	_____	_____	_____
Clothing	_____	_____	_____
Coin Collections	_____	_____	_____
Computers, etc.	_____	_____	_____
Furniture	_____	_____	_____
Furs	_____	_____	_____
Home Entertainment Equipment (CD players, stereos, televisions, VCRs, etc.)	_____	_____	_____
Home Furnishings (drapes, blankets, etc.)	_____	_____	_____

Jewelry	_____	_____	_____
Lighting Fixtures	_____	_____	_____
Motorcycles, etc.	_____	_____	_____
Paintings and Sculptures	_____	_____	_____
Pools, etc.	_____	_____	_____
Stamp Collections	_____	_____	_____
Tableware (glasses, plates, silverware, etc.)	_____	_____	_____
Tools, etc.	_____	_____	_____
Other	_____	_____	_____
Total Personal Property		$_____	$_____
Total Assets		$_____	$_____

within a few days; *illiquid* assets are the opposite: it could take months, even years to access that money.)

▶ Do you want to make that account grow as fast as possible to support your retirement?

If you're looking for an extremely safe investment that creates extra income while growing fast, forget it. You are asking the impossible. You may be able to find a blend of two out of the three, but not all three.

Finally, you should reassess your risk tolerance. You may find that because of your divorce, you have become more conservative in your investment outlook. Or you might feel more able to take risks now that you are not restrained by your former spouse.

Whatever the case, evaluate your risk profile before making any investment moves.

Keep in mind that, after a divorce, many people frequently have little money left over to invest if the breakup was bitter and protracted. But even if you end up with few assets, you should establish a disciplined savings program to get you back on your feet. Set aside each month a regular amount of money, whether it be $10 or $1,000+, in a bank account or mutual fund so that you can build a capital base.

If you end up with some assets, also establish a regular savings program, though you might be able to create a larger and more diversified portfolio than a less fortunate divorcee. If you are young, invest more aggressively in growth-oriented stocks or mutual funds. If you are elderly, you'll likely need to keep a majority of the money in income-producing vehicles, such as bonds, bond funds, or certificates of deposit (CDs). The next section covers investing options in more detail.

▶ Stop #3: Map Your Future Journey by Reassessing Your Investment Portfolio

The money triangle in Tollbooth 6.1 represents three key areas of your money and investment strategies. This is a simple illustration, but that simplicity is what can help you formulate your financial plans.

At the top of the triangle is *growth;* at the left, *income;* and at the right, *security.* (Here, *security* means the amount of risk you are comfortable with to achieve the other two components.) The closer you move toward growth, the further you move from income and security. If you were right in the middle of the triangle, you would have some income, some growth, and some security. Let's look at each of these options in more detail: this is Investing 101, but if you've never done it before, now's the time!

Route 1: On the Road to Very Secure but Limited Investments

Let's say you're not willing to take risks with your money. When it comes to investing, you want your money to be safe. After all, grandfather was wiped out during the Crash of '29. The only things that you would be willing to put

Tollbooth 6.1

The Money Triangle

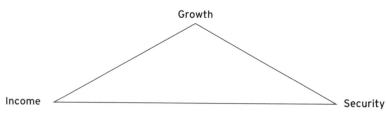

Growth

Income

Security

your money in are checking accounts, savings accounts, certificates of deposit, money market funds, and Treasury bills. Here are some ways to make these conservative vehicles work for you:

Checking accounts. Make sure your checking account pays interest. A non-interest-bearing checking account is the one place where there is a surprising amount of poorly used money. It's amazing how much money is left sitting in these accounts, not earning a penny in interest! Whatever funds you have, don't pooh-pooh interest on a few bucks. Every dime and dollar counts.

Now, having money sitting around not doing anything is a problem that a lot of people would welcome quite happily. But let's be practical: there is no sense in throwing good money away. And that's really what's happening when your money is not earning any interest, even for a day.

Savings accounts and certificates of deposit. These two types of accounts have something in common. Savings accounts need no explanation. When you buy a CD, as a depositor, you agree to place your funds with these institutions for a specific period. And because they guarantee you will get your money back with interest, the interest they offer you is much lower than what they charge someone for a loan. They then loan out your funds at a much higher rate. It can be anywhere from two to three percentage points above what you are currently receiving. Between loaning funds on deposit and credit card interest, the bulk of bank profits are made this way. But you're not interested in how your *bank* makes money; *you* want to make some money, so you should recognize that CDs pay more than a passbook savings account, but not a lot more.

Money market funds. These are a good "parking place" for monies until you decide what you want to do with them. You can withdraw money from them like a checking account, but it typically will have certain restrictions, such as only three withdrawals per month or a withdrawal must be for a minimum amount. It usually pays around a percentage higher than your typical passbook account.

Route 2: On the Road to Gaining Income from Your Investments

If you need your money to create extra cash each month, consider investing in bonds or bond mutual funds (which will be discussed in more detail later in this chapter).

Bonds come in several types: *corporate, municipals,* and *Treasuries.* They promise you safety of principal with interest. Looking back at the money triangle, the safer the bond, the lower the interest—which means *less income to you.*

Are all bonds safe? No. They range from U.S. Government bonds, guaranteed by the full faith and credit of the U.S. government to high yield (aka junk) bonds issued by companies with questionable strength.

There's a big difference between stocks and bonds; here's a simple way to compare them:

Bonds

▶ Principal is guaranteed.
▶ Rate of return is guaranteed.
▶ There will be no appreciation.
▶ You are loaning money to the company, municipality or government, or a creditor.

Stocks

▶ Principal is not guaranteed.
▶ Rate of return is not guaranteed.
▶ Value will go up or down with the success of the company.
▶ You are an owner of the company, a shareholder.

Corporate bonds. These are usually rated from C to AAA. The higher the rating—AAA is the highest—the higher the level of safety, though this still is not a guarantee, unless they are bonds issued by the U.S. government or an agency of the U.S. government or are insured, as some municipal bonds are. There are bonds that are rated as "junk," meaning that their safety and ability to pay regular interest payments are in jeopardy. Usually, investing in an A-rated or better bond will keep you in a margin of safety.

If you absolutely need income and you are adamant about safety of your money, you may want to invest in high-quality bonds. Their return on investment has been modest over the years in comparison with what stocks have generated, but they can play a part in creating a balanced portfolio along with investments that feature growth.

Municipal bonds. These are federal tax-free and, if they are issued within your resident state, they are also exempt from state taxes. Therefore, the higher your tax bracket, the more valuable your return. On the other hand, because this advantaged tax status increases the net yield, they pay lower interest rates than corporate bonds.

If you don't benefit significantly from the tax exemption, municipals may not be right for you. They are rated generally C+ to AAA, and can also be insured, which provides a AAA rating equivalent.

Treasury bonds. These are issued by and guaranteed by the U.S. government. Treasury bonds mature anywhere from 10 years to 20 years, Treasury notes mature from 1 to 10 years, and Treasury bills from 91 days to one year.

Bills, bonds, and notes are all safe investments with regard to return of principal. The federal government's backing makes them *fairly free* of risk of default, but that still doesn't guarantee that they won't oscillate in price and market value. They will—not with the wide discounting range of other bonds, but with a slight variance depending on rates and maturity date. They are very liquid, are generally sold for modest fees, if any, and are free of state and local (but not federal) taxes.

Route 3: On the Road to Growing Your Investments

Investing your money for growth means you're willing to leave the land of security and guarantees to look at higher risks with the hope of higher returns. Many financial investment products fit in this category. The most likely choices will be in *stocks* and *stock mutual funds.*

Stocks. Admittedly, the stock market can be a lucrative investment opportunity, but it can also be a bizarre circus, susceptible to daily whims and the emotions of participants. To invest and survive in the stock market, you must know and acknowledge both the risks and the remedies.

What is the market? Basically, it is a place where you can buy and sell ownership in a business. You are an owner, not a lender. Stock values change constantly. The price of a stock is determined by whatever someone else will pay for it. If a stock is listed on the New York Stock Exchange, or any of the other exchanges, prices will be negotiated on the floor of the exchange.

There are basically two types of stock: *growth* and *value* (or *income*). A growth company pays little, if any, cash dividends. These companies tend to be in newer, growing sectors of the economy and are likely to plow a large portion of earnings back into further growth opportunities, usually in research and development or expansion. Industries involving technology, communications, genetics, and health care offer classic examples.

Market prices of companies in these areas represent a substantial part of future prospects versus past performance. Stock value is expected to rise substantially over a period of time. The benefit to you is increased value, which is taxed at the time you elect to sell your shares.

Growth stocks are for growth, period. If you don't need cash income currently, but want to build a base where income can be generated at a later date, these are a viable option.

On the other hand, if you need income *now,* high-yield value stocks become one of your options. Stocks that distribute a large portion of the profits to stockholders in the form of a cash dividend rarely offer much in growth possibility. There are, of course, exceptions. Companies in more mature industries such as electric utilities, banks, and consumer durables tend to be value stocks.

Mutual funds. These investment options should be in every investor's portfolio. Even more, mutual funds can offer some significant benefits over individual stock purchases. A mutual fund is a pool of stock from many companies. Some of the companies are similar, some invest in income type investments, some spread their money into multiple industries. The fund can be a stock fund with 75 to 100 different stocks in it that are bought and sold by the manager of the fund. Or it may be a bond fund with many different bonds in it. Or you could have a blend of stocks and bonds to create growth and income in the same fund.

There are more than 15,000 mutual funds today. It can be quite confusing in deciding which one(s) you should invest in! Each fund has an objective that is stated clearly in its prospectus. It may be a group of high-tech companies for high growth. It may be a group of blue-chip stocks for solid, steady, slower, less risky growth. It may be a group of Treasury bonds for income. Research carefully so that you understand what you buying.

The advantage of buying a stock mutual fund for growth or a bond mutual fund for income is that you are hedging your bets against having all your money in just one or two stocks or one or two bonds. With a large pool of stocks in a growth fund, if one stock fails, the others can hold up the fund. The fund manager's job is to watch the market constantly and buy or sell as they seem prudent to meet the objective of the fund.

Mutual funds offer many advantages. One is expertise. If you are swamped and don't have the time or the skill to study and pick your own stocks, mutual funds offer professional management. It is not only acceptable but smart to get help if you don't have the knowledge.

Mutual funds allow you to "dollar cost average" and reinvest dividends and gains. *Dollar cost averaging* means putting the same amount of money into the same fund on a regular basis (monthly, quarterly, etc.). One certainty of the stock market is that it will fluctuate. Instead of fighting or fearing this key fact, put it to work for you.

For example, let's say you decide to put in $100 per month. When the share price of your fund is up, your $100 doesn't buy as many shares. But when the share price is down, your $100 buys more shares. It's like getting them on sale! And then when the share price moves back up again, you have more shares growing for you. Most funds provide a bank draft authorization so that the bank can automatically deduct the $100 from your account each month. We think of it as tithing to yourself. It's a good way to place yourself on "automatic," or cruise control: each month on a specific date, a set amount of money is transferred to your fund account. A forced type of investing/savings that becomes a habit!

> *You have the option of reinvesting dividends and capital gains or taking them in cash.*

You need to watch your mutual funds, just like any other investment. Most funds follow consistent investment strategies based on extensive research, primarily done by the fund's management. The managers decide when and what securities to buy or sell; give you the option of regular disbursements or automatic reinvestment of gains, dividends, or interest; and take care of the paperwork for IRS purposes at the end of the year.

With that said, do people lose money in funds? Yes, they have and will. Mutual funds carry risk, just as other investments do. In considering investing in a fund, you would be wise to make sure that the manager has at least five years' experience with a positive track record as measured against their peers. For more information visit http://www.morningstar.com or the Mutual Fund Education Alliance at http://www.mfea.com.

It is generally recommended that you reinvest all dividends and gains. This gives you the opportunity to speed up your compounding potential.

Money in the Glove Compartment: Maintaining a Liquidity Fund

You may be tempted to put all your cash into some type of investment, thinking that's the best way to get growth. Don't. Life is quite good at delivering the unexpected. You need a slush fund for any possible emergencies. Emergencies come in the form of new tires, medical care that insurance doesn't cover, cutbacks or layoffs at work, Mother Nature's destruction, flying somewhere for a funeral, or even having to bail someone out of jail.

> *Everyone needs a liquidity fund, monies that you can access within a couple of days.*

In general, it is strongly suggested that everyone have from three to six months' fixed expenses in your liquidity fund—i.e., your backup emergency fund. That way, if you have to take time to get another job, get well, grieve, or fix the roof, you'll be able to cover those expenses plus your everyday fixed ones (utilities, housing, food, and any ongoing bills) for a few months. Keep in mind, though, that this fund doesn't cover eating out, buying spiffy new clothes, or taking vacations.

▶ Stop #4: Get the Keys to the Car by Finalizing Property Transfers

So, you've had your day in court, and the divorce process is all over, right? Not so fast: once a divorce decree has been signed by the court, two major questions remain:

1. When does your marriage actually end? This can vary somewhat from state to state. In some states, the marriage is ended when the judge signs the decree. In other states, a certain period of time must pass before the marriage is ended. And in others, it may be ended when the judge rules in court, even before an order has been signed. It can all be confusing, so make sure your lawyer tells you exactly when your marriage is dissolved.

2. How and when will property be transferred? Your decree or agreement may require that certain personal property, such as furniture or jewelry,

Hazard!
Get It in Writing

Make sure you know when you are legally divorced.

If new insurance policies are to be established, account titles/ownership or beneficiaries changed, demand *written proof* that this has been done.

---

be physically transferred to the party to whom it has been awarded. And in the case of other assets, not only must the *physical* transfer take place, but the *paperwork* to transfer the title must also be accomplished.

Roadmap 6.4 offers a list of questions you should ask your attorney to help facilitate the transfer of property.

Travel Documents for Your New Solo Journey

Some property requires paperwork to complete the transfer; the following sections describe what you need to do for each type of property.

Real Estate. The divorce agreement or order may require that the title of real estate be changed to one party individually. In this case, you may need a deed and other documents (such as an appraisal or new title insurance).

You may encounter a document called a quitclaim deed. This is a type of deed in which the person who transfers an interest does not guarantee that the title belongs to the said person. In essence, the deed says, "If I have any interest in this property, and I'm not saying I do, I transfer it to you." Discuss with your lawyer if this will be enough in your case. If rental property is involved, a new lease or insurance may also be necessary. Check on insurance coverage for your residence too.

Vehicles. Titles for automobiles, boats, airplanes, or motorcycles may need to be changed. And don't forget to arrange for the transfer of insurance, which may mean finding a new company.

If you were unlucky and didn't get the car in your divorce agreement, you will have to buy or lease a car of your own, which may be difficult if your income has been reduced. Therefore, you should finance an inexpensive, basic model that will get you where you need to go without many frills.

Roadmap 6.4

12 Financial Questions to Ask Before You Leave Your Lawyer

1. When is the divorce decree effective?

2. When will I get a copy of it?

3. If support payments are ordered, what is due and when? (And whether you are the one *making* payments or the one *receiving* them, set up a system for tracking payments.)

4. What documents will I receive showing that property transfers have been made?

5. Who is responsible for preparing and filing each document?

6. What am I required to do under the order?

7. What am I entitled to receive under the order?

8. How much do I owe you? Will there be additional costs?

9. When can I pick up my personal property? *or* When will it be delivered?

10. What should I do if the order is not followed? Will you still be available to help me?

11. Who will pay your fees if I have to sue for enforcement of the order?

12. Can you look at my estate plan and tell me what I should do now, or can you refer me to someone who can?

Insurance. For life insurance, it may be necessary to change a beneficiary, and new insurance may be part of the deal. You should reevaluate your life insurance needs. In many cases, only one spouse in a marriage works outside the home, usually the husband, and he is covered by a policy aside from that provided by an employer. After a divorce, he probably will remove his ex-wife as the policy's beneficiary. Any children of the marriage will likely remain as beneficiaries, at least contingent, if not primary, however.

Therefore, if you are a divorced woman with custody of the children, whether or not you work outside the home, purchase an insurance policy on your life. If you were to die while your children were young, they would need the life insurance proceeds to assist the children's guardian in maintaining the standard of living to which they've become accustomed, and to get them through school and on the road to self-sufficiency.

Health insurance coverage is critical as well (refer back to Chapter 4 for more information on health insurance). For example, if you were a nonemployed spouse covered under your employed spouse's policy, you need to take steps with that employer to arrange for continued coverage after the divorce. Check this carefully, because there may be strict time limits for the transfer.

After a divorce, most people have rights to receive health insurance coverage under COBRA for 36 months. Coverage under COBRA is not automatic, however. You must tell your ex-spouse's employer within 60 days of the date you are notified of your rights that you plan to continue the health insurance policy. If you receive no such notification from the insurance company within a few weeks after the divorce is finalized, inquire further. If you let this 60-day period elapse, you lose your COBRA rights.

If you are getting a divorce or are already divorced and currently employed, study your company's employee benefits even more carefully than before, and maximize whatever options your employer provides. This means you should participate in retirement savings plans, health and disability insurance plans, and educational scholarship programs. Your employers may also offer employee assistance programs, which might help you overcome the emotional and financial turmoil of your divorce. Perhaps you relied on your spouse to look after your employee benefits while you were married. After the divorce, you are responsible for making the most of the benefits that your employer offers.

Hazard!
Watch the Clock

After your divorce, continued health care for the nonemployee spouse probably is available, but strict time limits for conversion may apply.

Take care of this as soon as possible, to ensure you have the coverage you need.

Also, you should try as soon as possible to line up new health insurance through your own employer and, if that is not available, possibly through any group of which you are a member, such as a trade association. Buying health insurance individually can be extremely expensive. But you *can't afford not* to have health insurance.

As discussed in Chapter 4, if you are to be the beneficiary of a life insurance policy, it is far better for *you* to own the policy and pay the premiums than for your ex-spouse to do so and promise not to change the policy. An insurance company will not take on the burden of notifying you if there is a change from what the court ordered, so you could end up with no coverage and not know about it if the change was made since your last inquiry to the company. Don't let this happen: transfer ownership of your ex-spouse's insurance *now*.

If you work, it is important to purchase adequate disability insurance coverage, if you don't already have sufficient coverage. If you get seriously injured or ill and can not work for an extended period of time, you will need the income that a disability policy provides.

Purchase a disability insurance policy that is guaranteed renewable and offers an appropriate elimination period—that is, the time you must wait before you begin receiving payments. For example, if payments are delayed six months, make sure you have accumulated enough emergency savings and/or a short-term disability policy (this is the "liquidity fund" described earlier in this chapter) to tide you over until the checks start flowing. The most inexpensive way to buy disability insurance is through your employer, though you can also buy it from most major life insurance companies. Visit http://www.insure.com for more information.

If you receive your home or apartment as part of the divorce settlement, make sure you update your homeowner's insurance. First, remove your ex-spouse's name from the insurance policy. Because your ex-spouse may have taken many possessions from your home, take a fresh household inventory to assess whether you have adequate insurance coverage. (Keep in mind that you may need *less* insurance coverage on the contents if your spouse took many of your household goods—which may be small comfort, but at least is less of a financial burden.) Roadmap 6.5 can help you take an inventory of all your household possessions. If you rent, purchase a renter's policy to cover the replacement cost of your possessions.

Roadmap 6.5

Household Inventory Worksheet

Article and Description	Purchase Price	Replacement Cost	Total Purchase Cost	Total Replacement Cost
Bathrooms				
Carpets/Rugs	$_____	$_____		
Clothes Hampers	_____	_____		
Curtains	_____	_____		
Dressing Tables	_____	_____		
Electrical Appliances	_____	_____		
Lighting Fixtures	_____	_____		
Linens	_____	_____		
Scales	_____	_____		
Shower Curtains	_____	_____		
Other	_____	_____		
Total for Bathrooms			$_____	$_____
Bedrooms				
Beds/Mattresses	$_____	$_____		
Books/Bookcases	_____	_____		
Carpets/Rugs	_____	_____		
Chairs	_____	_____		
Clocks	_____	_____		
Clothing	_____	_____		
Curtains/Drapes	_____	_____		
Desks	_____	_____		
Dressers	_____	_____		
Lamps	_____	_____		
Mirrors	_____	_____		
Plants	_____	_____		
Records/Tapes/CDs	_____	_____		
Stereos/Radios	_____	_____		
Tables	_____	_____		
Televisions	_____	_____		
Wall Hangings/Pictures	_____	_____		
Wall Units	_____	_____		
Other	_____	_____		
Total for Bedrooms			$_____	$_____
Dining Room				
Buffets	$_____	$_____		
Carpets/Rugs	_____	_____		
Chairs	_____	_____		

Article and Description	Purchase Price	Replacement Cost	Total Purchase Cost	Total Replacement Cost
Dining Room (cont'd)				
China	_____	_____		
Clocks	_____	_____		
Curtains/Drapes	_____	_____		
Glassware	_____	_____		
Lamps/Fixtures	_____	_____		
Silverware	_____	_____		
Tables	_____	_____		
Wall Hangings/Pictures	_____	_____		
Other	_____	_____		
Total for Dining Room			$_____	$_____
Garage/Basement/Attic				
Furniture	$_____	$_____		
Ladders	_____	_____		
Lawn Mowers	_____	_____		
Luggage	_____	_____		
Shovels	_____	_____		
Snowblowers	_____	_____		
Sports Equipment	_____	_____		
Sprinklers/Hoses	_____	_____		
Tools/Supplies	_____	_____		
Toys	_____	_____		
Washer/Dryer	_____	_____		
Wheelbarrows	_____	_____		
Work Benches	_____	_____		
Other	_____	_____		
Total for Garage/Basement/Attic			$_____	$_____
Kitchen				
Buffets	$_____	$_____		
Cabinets	_____	_____		
Chairs	_____	_____		
Clocks	_____	_____		
Curtains	_____	_____		
Dishes	_____	_____		
Dishwasher	_____	_____		
Disposal/Trash Compactor	_____	_____		
Food/Supplies	_____	_____		
Freezer	_____	_____		
Glassware	_____	_____		
Lighting Fixtures	_____	_____		
Refrigerator	_____	_____		

Article and Description	Purchase Price	Replacement Cost	Total Purchase Cost	Total Replacement Cost
Kitchen (cont'd)				
Pots/Pans	___	___		
Radio/Television	___	___		
Small Appliances	___	___		
Stove	___	___		
Tables	___	___		
Washer/Dryer	___	___		
Other	___	___		
Total for Kitchen			$___	$___
Living Room				
Books/Bookcases	$___	$___		
Carpets/Rugs	___	___		
Chairs	___	___		
Clocks	___	___		
Curtains/Drapes	___	___		
Desks	___	___		
Lamps	___	___		
Mirrors	___	___		
Musical Instruments	___	___		
Plants	___	___		
Records/Tapes/CDs	___	___		
Sofas	___	___		
Stereo/Radio	___	___		
Tables	___	___		
Television	___	___		
Wall Hangings/Pictures	___	___		
Wall Units	___	___		
Other	___	___		
Total for Living Room			$___	$___
Porch/Patio				
Carpets/Rugs	$___	$___		
Chairs	___	___		
Lamps	___	___		
Outdoor Cooking Equipment	___	___		
Outdoor Furniture	___	___		
Plants/Planters	___	___		
Tables	___	___		
Other	___	___		
Total for Porch/Patio			$___	$___
TOTAL HOUSEHOLD			$___	$___

Stocks, Bonds, Mutual Funds, Bank Accounts, and Certificates of Deposit. A change of ownership of these accounts and money instruments may be necessary, or, at a minimum, the method of ownership and beneficiary designations needs to be changed. For some cash instruments, such as *bearer bonds,* it is only necessary to physically transfer possession. For savings bonds, other paperwork may be required.

Business. If there is to be a transfer of an interest in a business, certain formalities will be required, depending on the form of the business. If the business is a corporation and stock is owned, a transfer from one spouse to the other may be needed, or from both to one. If one spouse is an officer of the corporation, there will have to be a formal withdrawal from that office, as well as notices to the secretary of state for the state in which the business is incorporated. And if the business is operating under a trade name, notices may also be required to the secretary of state. Whether it's your business or your ex-spouse's, make sure you engage and supervise a corporate attorney to effect all these transfers and handle all these notifications.

> *If you do not have current estate planning documents in place, prepare them now! At the same time, don't forget about ancillary documents such as health care directives, living will, limited power of attorney for financial decision-making, and funeral directives.*

Debts. Notify your and your ex-spouse's creditors of new billing addresses; you may also need new payment coupons. This is also a great time to establish new lines of credit (as discussed in detail in Chapter 5). You should destroy old joint credit cards and close all joint accounts if you have not already done so. Notify creditors who gave you joint credit that you are no longer married to your ex-spouse and no longer responsible for their debts. And don't forget to notify the utility companies.

Wills. You will probably need to completely rewrite or significantly modify your existing will. At the very least, review and modify your will with an experienced estate attorney.

Your estate planning attorney may recommend a living trust. A living trust speeds up the process of transferring your assets to your heirs when

Hazard!

What You Don't Know Can Cost You Plenty

Seek the advice of a knowledgeable tax expert before you begin to transfer assets from one name to the other.

you die. Appendix B lists several Web sites that offer information about wills and trusts.

Trusts. If you already have a trust, you will probably need to change beneficiaries or terms of payment and management. A new trust may be needed to comply with terms of the agreement or order. Again, see Appendix B for Web sites that offer more information on trusts.

Promissory Notes. Because of the terms of the divorce agreement or order, you or your ex-spouse may be required to execute a promissory note. For example, this may be needed if the court ordered one of you to pay the other a certain amount of money, and the debtor party does not have that much cash on hand. You should either have the notes collateralized (in case of a bankruptcy), backed by an insurance policy (in case of death), or both. Promissors should be drafted by your attorney.

Income Taxes. At a minimum, you need to clarify your filing status for your next tax return. There may also be a refund to deal with, and your divorce agreement or order should say who it belongs to. And if your spouse was to cover you in case of a tax bill in the future, make sure the proper document has been prepared to protect you.

Also, you should know what taxes may result from all of these property transfers. The general rule is that the increased value of property transferred between spouses as part of a divorce is *not taxable* at the time of the transfer. The tax issue will arise when the property is later sold or transferred. (Refer back to Chapter 2 for more information on the tax implications of property transfers.)

Retirement Accounts. Ideally, the retirement division order was prepared for signing at the time of the divorce. But if it was not, don't delay on this

—the results of procrastination can be devastating. To reiterate, if no proper order is in place and the employee dies, the nonemployee spouse will end up with *nothing* from the retirement plan—and the retirement may have been the most valuable asset of the marriage. A particularly terrible result can take place if the employee remarries and then dies before an order is in place. In this case, the new spouse will receive all of the survivor benefits. Refer back to Chapter 3 for a detailed review of information on retirement benefits and pensions.

Social Security. If you were married for at least 10 years and did not work outside the house, qualify for individual Social Security benefits, or were the lower-earning spouse, you will be able to collect up to half of your spouse's benefits, presuming they qualify for Social Security. It will not reduce your spouse's benefits. If you remarry, are married for at least 10 years, and get divorced from the second spouse, you can choose between ex-spouse #1 and ex-spouse #2's benefit, or opt for your own benefit, whichever is higher. Again, it will not diminish your ex's benefit.

The average length of marriage that ends in divorce is 9.6 years! Protect yourself. If you are considering signing those final papers after nine and a half years of marriage, you may want to hang in there another six months!

▶ On the Road Again with Someone New: Financial Issues to Consider if You Remarry

When you're just finalizing a divorce, you may not be able to even think about getting involved with someone new or ever marrying again. But the simple fact is that many people do remarry, and many bring children to that new family unit. And that may happen sooner than you think. Therefore, it's worth a few minutes to think about some of the financial issues and decisions that accompany such an adventure—now, while you're not caught up in the throes of a new romance.

Discuss the Rules of the Road: Consider a Prenuptial Agreement

The following sections describe scenarios where you should at least consider drawing up a prenuptial agreement.

If You and Your New Spouse Are Both Young, with Equal Assets. A pre-nup protects young people in the early stages of promising careers, where each has some assets and wants to protect these, as well as their careers, as separate property.

If You and Your New Spouse Are Both Young, with Unequal Assets. This scenario applies to people of middle age or younger, where one of you already has, or will probably acquire, substantial assets and wants to protect these assets as separate property, while reasonably providing for the needs of the marriage, as well as the spouse and any children if there is a divorce.

If One of You Is Young and the Other Much Older, with Unequal Assets. This scenario applies to a couple with large differences in age and wealth, where the older party has substantial wealth which they want to preserve for their estate, and also want to provide for disability or incapacity.

If You and Your New Spouse Are Both Older, with Unequal Assets. This scenario applies to an elderly couple, where one party has substantially fewer assets than the other, and where both want to:

▶ protect their separate property,
▶ provide for a comfortable lifestyle during the marriage, and
▶ reasonably provide for the spouse with fewer assets upon death or divorce.

If You and Your New Spouse Are Both Older, with Equal Assets. This scenario applies to older people with similar assets who want to protect their property as separate, yet provide an arrangement by which they can live in line with their wealth.

Roadmap 6.6 lists 13 topics you should consider in a prenuptial agreement.

▶ Getting Around a Roadblock: How to Buy a New Home If Your Credit Is Ruined

Chapter 5 discussed how to handle credit problems if you're on your own, but getting remarried introduces other situations—most typically, buying a new house with your new spouse. If your credit is terrible (either because of your own mismanagement during your previous marriage or after the

Roadmap 6.6

13 Topics to Cover in a Prenuptial Agreement, If You Get Remarried*

1. How income will be used from the separate property of each spouse.
2. How joint property will be acquired and used.
3. Premarital and postmarital ownership by one party.
4. How pensions will be paid out if one of the parties dies.
5. What to do if one party becomes incapacitated or disabled.
6. Intentions of having children.
7. Rearing of children from a prior marriage.
8. Financial responsibilities toward parents.
9. Responsibilities for debts acquired before and during the marriage.
10. Filing status for income tax returns.
11. Provisions in wills and trusts.
12. Spousal support if there is a divorce.
13. Property division if there is a divorce.

*Exact contents will depend on circumstances of the parties.

divorce, or because your ex-spouse ruined it), there's still hope for you—if your new spouse has good credit.

You do need to be very careful when you are applying for any new credit, whether it be for a credit card or a mortgage. The way the credit system works when you are applying for new credit jointly, your negative credit will not allow you to qualify, even with your new spouse's excellent credit. This is especially true if your income is higher than your new spouse's.

A credit grantor will look at the wage earner who is making the highest salary to determine an approval or denial. If *your* income is higher than your new spouse's, the credit grantor will evaluate the application on *your* creditworthiness rather than your spouse's.

Therefore, the best thing to do is to have your new spouse apply for new credit. Once your spouse has been approved, the spouse can request another credit card for you with your name on it; this can be either a joint or user card. Your spouse will be responsible for making the payments, but this will help you add new credit to your credit report.

If you are applying for a mortgage, wait until the new credit is seasoned for at least a year. Then, your new spouse should apply for a credit card solely —not with you as a joint applicant. If your spouse is approved for the mortgage, your spouse will be the one solely responsible for the payments, and only your spouse's name will be recorded on the title. Then, after the loan is closed, your spouse can file a quitclaim deed adding you to the title. It must be recorded with the county recorder's office. Also, after you have re-established your credit history, you can refinance your home jointly.

▶ Moving on Down the Road: Summing Up

Once you've addressed all the issues in this chapter, you should be well on the road to a new, more secure financial life. Remember, you should develop a new financial plan, consider hiring a financial advisor to help you, assess your current assets and establish new savings and investing goals, rebalance your investment portfolio, and transfer property as needed and make sure all the paperwork is complete. Then you can start to think about new financial issues for happier times. This chapter's advice and recommendations should set you well on course to financial stability. Bon voyage!

Appendix A

An Itinerary

Here's a quick review of what to do, as you set out on the road to getting your finances in order when you're getting divorced:

▶ Stop 1: Decide Whether You Want To Hire A Divorce Attorney or Work With A Mediator Or Arbitrator

▶ Hire your own attorney: you and your spouse can't "share" one attorney.

▶ Get qualified referrals for several attorneys; make sure they're experienced in divorce cases; and interview them carefully before hiring anyone.

▶ Pay attention to personality factors when choosing an attorney: you should be comfortable with the person representing you and your interests, so don't ignore your gut instincts.

▶ Consider working with a legal clinic instead of a single lawyer—if your case is simple. But don't try a "do-it-yourself" divorce: you *need* good advice and counsel during this process.

▶ Understand your attorney's billing process so there are no unpleasant surprises about the cost of representation.

▶ Communicate openly and learn how to work effectively with your attorney—and with your attorney's staff, who can be extremely helpful in facilitating your divorce.

▶ Know the difference between arbitration and mediation before you choose either of these routes: both involve a neutral third party, but there are significant differences in how your divorce will be decided.

► Stop 2: Understand What's Involved In Dividing Up Your Property—It's Probably More Than You Thought

► Know how your property could be divided if you live in a *community property* state, an *equitable distribution* state, or an *equal distribution* state.

► Go on a "scavenger hunt" to make sure you've accounted for everything that might constitute marital property—before it walks out the door of your home.

► Gather up all your financial records—payroll stubs, bank statements, check registers, deeds, titles, insurance policies, tax returns, and prenuptial agreements (and more: your attorney will need these to determine a fair division of property).

► Learn how to deal with marital debt, credit problems that may linger after your divorce, even bankruptcy.

► Find out how much your property is worth: this includes your house, savings account, stock or other investments, jewelry, artwork, antiques and collectibles, home furnishings, and any other valuables.

► Decide what to do with your home: sell and split the proceeds, have one spouse buy out the other, or own the home jointly—and understand the tax implications of each.

► Don't ignore the assets that accompany each spouse's job: insurance (life, health, disability insurance), Social Security, stock options, and pension and retirement plans: most of these have to be divvied up, too.

► Determine the value of "PHTS/PWTS": putting your husband or wife through school. This cost should be assessed and included in a divorce settlement.

► Find out how to calculate the value of a family business so you can divide it up and go your separate ways.

▶ Stop 3: Get What You're Entitled To, In Terms Of Your Share Of Pensions And Retirement Benefits

▶ Know the different ways you can receive money from your ex-spouse's retirement benefits: the *buy-out* or *cash-out* method (a lump sum) vs. the *deferred division* or *future share* method.

▶ Understand how different types of retirement plans also affect payment: defined-contribution plans vs. defined-benefit plans.

▶ Anticipate common mistakes that divorce lawyers make when divvying up pensions—and avoid them by bringing in a qualified financial specialist.

▶ Learn how to transfer assets so you don't get taxed unnecessarily in the process.

▶ Update your own financial plans for retirement, now that you have only one income: reassess your savings, investments, and expenses—be prepared!

▶ Stop 4: Make Sure You Get What You Need In Terms Of Alimony and Child Support

▶ Know what criteria are required for paying or receiving alimony: financial need, ability to pay, the length of your marriage, your previous lifestyle, and the age and health status of both you and your ex.

▶ Understand the different types of alimony: rehabilitative (i.e., financial help until the receiving spouse is able to fend for one's self) and modifiable vs. non-modifiable (where alimony payments can change as your and your ex's financial situations change).

▶ Be clear on all the tax implications of alimony payments: how payments must be made, what's deductible and what isn't, when it can end, and other considerations.

▶ Update all your insurance (life, health, disability). Make sure you (and your kids, if you have children) are covered under your own policies and, if appropriate, under your ex-spouse's.

▶ Factor in child support, if applicable. Know the criteria for determining the amount; understand the guidelines and tax implications (child support is *never* deductible, but you do need to know which ex-spouse can claim exemptions); and know how to enforce it through wage garnishment and other ways.

▶ Stop 5: Know Your Financial Rights During The Divorce Process, and Begin To Adjust Your Financial Situation For Your Post-Divorce Life

▶ Review your expenses to accommodate a new solo lifestyle—keeping in mind that you and your ex will now be supporting *two* households, with the concomitant two sets of bills. Learn how to reduce your expenses, if necessary.

▶ Re-evaluate your standard of living, and consider hiring a financial advisor to help you make necessary changes. Recognize that you may need to downscale your lifestyle.

▶ Don't swap emotional misery for financial misery, and don't do anything rash: don't raid bank accounts, and don't spend wildly just before your divorce. You'll end up paying later—and regretting it!

▶ Beware of common credit-card disasters—both yours and your ex's, which you may inherit. These can last even longer than your marriage did, if you're not careful! Protect your credit and know what to do if your ex-spouse ruined your credit or the IRS comes after you.

▶ Stop 6: Revise Your Financial Plans For Your Post-Divorce Future

▶ Consider hiring a financial advisor—and know what questions to ask before you do.

▶ Review your debts, assets, and budget for this next phase of your life.

▶ Reassess your short- and long-term financial goals—and how you can meet them.

▶ Reevaluate your investment portfolio: rebalance, if necessary, how your money is allocated in savings, checking, CDs, money-market funds, various types of bonds, stocks, annuities, mutual funds, and retirement accounts.

▶ Make sure you have some "liquid" money—an easily accessible emergency fund, in case you become ill or lose your job.

▶ Finalize all property transfers with your ex-spouse, for real estate, vehicles, insurance, investments, family business matters, debts, estate planning documents, income tax considerations, and retirement accounts.

▶ Start thinking—even though it's way early—about financial issues if you remarry: for example, consider a prenuptial agreement.

When you're on the road to getting divorced, it can be a difficult journey. But if you map the financial aspects well, that should make your trip easier. We hope this book has helped you.

Appendix B

The Best of *Surviving Divorce*:
A Resource Guide

▶ Bibliography

The following books were used as resources for this book. In addition, there are lists of other books and Web sites that offer more detailed information on some of the topics covered in this book. We hope you find all these resources useful.

Briles, Judith et al. *The Dollars and Sense of Divorce*. Chicago: Dearborn Trade Publishing, 1998.

Garrett, Sheryl. *Just Give Me the Answers*. Chicago: Dearborn Trade Publishing, 2004

Goodman, Jordan E. *Everyone's Money Book,* 3rd ed. Chicago: Dearborn Trade Publishing, 2001.

McNaughton, Deborah. *All About Credit*. Chicago: Dearborn Trade Publishing, 1999.

Ventura, John. *The Will Kit,* 2nd ed. Chicago: Dearborn Trade Publishing, 2002.

▶ Recommended Additional Books and Web Sites with Useful Information

For Chapter 1, on attorneys, mediation, arbitration

A Guide to Divorce Mediation by Gary Friedman, Workman Publishing, 1993.

For Chapter 2, on dividing up property

To find a business appraiser—contact any of the following organizations:

- ▶ American Society of Appraisers (ASA)
- ▶ International Society of Appraisers (ISA)
- ▶ American Association of Appraisers (AAA)
- ▶ Institute of Business Appraisers (IBA)
- ▶ Certified Business Appraiser (CBA): CBAs must pass a rigorous exam and submit their appraisals for review by a committee of experienced peers.

To find a real estate appraiser for your house, call your local Board of Realtors® and ask for the average sale period in your area and price range to help guide you.

For Chapter 3, on pensions and retirement benefits

To find out how much you deserve in Social Security benefits after your divorce call the Social Security Administration at 800-772-1213; http://www.ssa.gov.

For Chapter 5, on managing expenses and credit

To check your credit report, contact one of the three national credit bureaus:

1. Equifax. Telephone: 800-685-1111; http://www.equifax.com
2. Experian. Telephone: 800-682-7654; http://www.experian.com/product/consumer
3. Trans Union. Telephone: 800-916-8800; http://www.tuc.com

For professional financial advice, contact:

- ▶ The Institute for Divorce Financial Analysts: http://www.institutedfa.com.

For more information on Social Security retirement benefits from your ex-spouse see:

- ▶ The Social Security Web site: http://www.ssa.gov.

For Chapter 6, on financial planning

To check out financial advisors and find out if any securities complaints have been filed against them, contact the following:

▶ The National Association of Security Dealers (NASD):
1735 K St., N.W.
Washington, DC 20006
Telephone: 202-778-8000
http://www.nasd.com

▶ The Securities and Exchange Commission (SEC):
405 Fifth St., N.W.
Washington, DC 20549
Telephone: 202-942-7040
http://www.sec.gov

To find an advisor visit:

▶ http://www.GarrettPlanningNetwork.com

For information about wills and trusts, see the following Web sites:

▶ http://www.nolo.com
▶ http://www.lawdepot.com

Index

Share the message!

Bulk discounts
Discounts start at only 10 copies and range from 30% to 55% off retail price based on quantity.

Custom publishing
Private label a cover with your organization's name and logo. Or, tailor information to your needs with a custom pamphlet that highlights specific chapters.

Ancillaries
Workshop outlines, videos, and other products are available on select titles.

Dynamic speakers
Engaging authors are available to share their expertise and insight at your event.

Call Dearborn Trade Special Sales at 1-800-621-9621, ext. 4444, or e-mail trade@dearborn.com.

Dearborn™
Trade Publishing
A **Kaplan Professional** Company